new approaches to
behavioral objectives

ISSUES AND INNOVATIONS IN EDUCATION

Consulting Editor
JOSEPH C. BENTLEY
The University of Utah

Expanding the Self: Personal Growth for Teachers—
*Angelo V. Boy and Gerald J. Pine, University of
New Hampshire*

Changing Student Behavior: A New Approach to
Discipline—*Duane Brown, West Virginia University*

Classroom Evaluation for Teachers—*Henry Dizney,
University of Oregon*

Compensatory Programming: The Acid Test of
American Education—*Joe L. Frost, The University
of Texas at Austin, and G. Thomas Rowland, The
Institute for Epistemic Studies*

Educational Media and the Teacher—*John B. Haney,
University of Illinois at Chicago Circle, and
Eldon J. Ullmer, The Florida State University*

Motivation—*Ivan L. Russell, Southern Illinois
University—Edwardsville*

Group Processes in the Classroom—*Richard A.
Schmuck, University of Oregon, and Patricia A.
Schmuck*

Encouraging Creativity in the Classroom—*E. Paul
Torrance, University of Georgia*

New Approaches to Behavioral Objectives—
Richard W. Burns, University of Texas—El Paso

new approaches to behavioral objectives

Richard W. Burns

University of Texas El Paso

WM. C. BROWN COMPANY PUBLISHERS

Dubuque, Iowa

Contents

Preface vii

1. Introduction 1

2. Is It a Goal or an Objective? 3

3. Is It a Terminal Behavioral Objective or an Instructional
   Objective? 5
   Criterion Test—Sections 2 and 3 8

4. More About Objectives 10
   Criterion Test 21

5. What Kind of an Objective Do I Have? 22
   Criterion Test 35

6. More About Affective Behaviors 37
   Criterion Test 47

7. Covert and Overt Behaviors or Primary and Secondary
   Behaviors 49
   Criterion Test 54

8. What Is the Difference Between an Open and Closed
   Objective? 57
   Criterion Test 63

9. How Do I Know My Objective Is Good? 66
   Criterion Test 74

10. How Do I Use My Objective? 76
    Criterion Test 81

11. What Are Experience Objectives? 83
    Criterion Test 85

12. Show Me Some Examples 87

Appendix A 97
  A-1. Answers to Criterion Test—Sections 2 and 3 97
  A-2. Key to Self Check Test—Section 4 97
  A-3. Answers to Self Check Test 97
  A-4. Answers to Self Check Test 98
  A-5. Answers to Criterion Test—Section 5 98
  A-6. Answers to Criterion Test—Section 7 99
  A-7. Answers to Criterion Test—Section 8 100
  A-8. Answers to Criterion Test—Section 10 100
  A-9. Answers to Criterion Test—Section 11 101

Appendix B The Nine Classes of Behaviors with Synoptic,
            Related or Subcategory Terms and Associated
            Behaviors (Actions) 102

Appendix C Simplified Taxonomy for Educational Objectives 107

Index 117

Preface

Before one can write a book, design instructional materials, prepare a course of study, plan units of instruction, or develop daily lesson plans he must have goals and objectives in mind. This volume deals extensively with the objectives for instructional settings—their selection, creation, writing, evaluation, and use.

Education is rapidly becoming criterion-referenced or behaviorally-oriented at all levels from preschool through university. Teacher training itself is being performance-based. All of these trends demand that the individuals involved, whether professors, teacher trainees, public school teachers, or school administrators, must be skillful in the development and analysis of objectives. It is my hope that this volume, because of its self-instructional features, will assist you in acquiring all the skill you will need in writing and evaluating objectives. What this book cannot do is provide you with extensive practice or a situation requiring the application of your new skill.

A how-to-do-it type of book, it is designed for use in college and university curriculum and methods courses and also for in-service training of educators at all levels. It has intentionally been written in less technical language than that usually found in textbooks, and its format styled to allow you to proceed comfortably at your own pace while learning. There are self-administered, self-check evaluations, and practical exercises to help you learn by doing as you proceed.

By learning to create and properly express objectives you will be developing an extension of your ability to communicate and plan. Objectives, with few exceptions, should be made known to your students so that they can terminate their instruction with the ability to perform—that is, learners should be able to prove to you, by doing, that they have achieved the objectives as you have written them.

We are entering an era of accountability in teaching in which teachers are being asked to furnish evidence that learning has occurred. Properly designed objectives will be the "key" which will enable you to furnish evidence that learning has taken place. When students can perform those things they set out to learn you can be assured that your teaching has been successful. This text will help you to become more successful in producing changes in your students. *As students change they are learning!*

Special attention has been given to affective objectives, an area of concern to many teachers. In addition to learning how to write objectives there are sections on evaluating objectives, how to use them in the classroom, and a special section providing examples of what the author considers to be good objectives. The text is comprehensive in its treatment of all aspects of objectives and their use.

1

Introduction

GOAL: To make you interested or concerned enough to proceed.

Scarcely anyone would argue against having goals for instruction, nor do teachers balk at talking about the purpose of their teaching. However, as much as we hate to admit it, the stated goals and purposes of education tend to be rather useless, vague, and general expressions having only limited meaning to educators.

Educational theorists do not quarrel with such broad goals as:

1. Developing the whole child.
2. Aiding in character development.
3. Teaching good citizenship.
4. Developing leadership.
5. Promoting good health and physical fitness.
6. Developing appreciation for art and beauty.
7. Encouraging the child to think.

They do claim though, that such broad goals are relatively useless when it comes to developing units, constructing curricula, creating instructional modules, selecting teaching aids, suggesting instructional activities, and creating criteria tests. The reason broad statements are less than useful is that they do not specify exactly what students (learners) are to do at the termination of learning. The need is for more functional statements of objectives, met by developing *specific, behavioral objectives* sometimes variously called, instructional objectives, terminal behaviors, performance goals, performance objectives, specific objectives, and very frequently just plain "objectives."

Now the idea of behavioral objectives is far from new, lists of objectives having been developed in the 1920's.[1] What is new is the in-

---

1. Franklin Babbit, *How to Make a Curriculum* (Boston: Houghton Mifflin Company, 1924).

creased realization that the quality of instruction, the quality of instructional materials, and the quality of achievement tests really demand that behavioral objectives all be set forth prior to instruction. And, even more shocking to teachers is the fact that they are being asked to write (develop) objectives for the very subjects that they teach.

No one seems to take kindly to new things—the new is somehow suspect—and in the case of behavioral objectives, setting them up can be ego deflating. That is, teachers hesitate to admit that they don't already know what they are teaching—in fact, many teachers are firmly convinced that what they are doing is very correct, helpful, and useful in its entirety. This type of reaction is very common and by no means confined to teachers—that which is new or unknown commonly tends to cause reluctance, hesitancy, even fear, in those who are to deal with it.

This text is designed to overcome any reluctance or hesitancy to deal with behavioral objectives. Learning what they are, how to write them, and how to use them is rewarding and he who *masters* the skill will become a better teacher.

2

Is It A Goal
or an Objective?

INSTRUCTIONAL OBJECTIVE: *Learner is to distinguish between goals and objectives, and know the terms goal and objective so that he can identify goals or objectives when presented with them.*

Objectives can be written, stated, and used in several different ways. Various authors use the term "objective" and several adjectival words connected with it to mean a variety of things. For this reason it is necessary, in order to understand this text, to know how the various terms are used in the sections which follow. If you see these terms used by other authorities in other ways you will probably be able to deduce their meaning by the context in which the terms are used.

Goals. Goals are statements of broad, general outcomes of instruction and they do not state or convey meaning in a behavioral sense—they *do not tell* what the learner is to *do* at the end of instruction.

Examples of goals:
1. The learner is to develop skill
2. The learner is to gain an appreciation of art
3. To develop leadership
4. For aiding in character development

Goals are:
1. broad, encompassing terms
2. sometimes expressed from the learner's point of view (see 1 and 2 above)
3. sometimes expressed from the teacher's point of view (see 3 and 4 above)

4. when listed, usually few in number
5. not expressed in behavioral terms

Objectives. Objectives are relatively specific statements of learning outcomes expressed frequently, but not always, in terms of the student.

Examples of objectives:
1. The learner is to identify the twelve cranial nerves
2. The learner is to list the fifty states in the United States
3. The learner is to be able to type a business letter
4. To show the students how to operate a 35-mm slide projector

Objectives are:
1. specific rather than broad
2. sometimes expressed from the learner's point-of-view (as 1, 2, and 3 above)
3. sometimes expressed from the teacher's point-of-view (see 4 above)
4. when listed, rather numerous (not demonstrated above).

At this point you should be able to distinguish between a goal (broad statement) and an objective (a relatively specific statement).

Which of the following are goals and which are objectives? Check **G** for *goal* and **O** for *objectives:*

1. Good health and physical fitness   (G)__ (O)__
2. To describe the theoretical structures of the   (G)__ (O)__
   Hydrogen atom
3. Appreciation of family living   (G)__ (O)__
4. To tell how a first class lever works   (G)__ (O)__
5. The learner is to gain skill in some vocational   (G)__ (O)__
   trade
6. The learner is to gain skill in using a band saw (G)__ (O)__

Check yourself now. If you said 1, 3, and 5 were goals (the odd numbered ones) you are *right!* The even numbered ones are objectives. If you did not select properly, may we suggest that you reread pages 3 and 4 about goals and objectives.

3

Is It a Terminal Behavior Objective or an Instructional Objective?

INSTRUCTIONAL OBJECTIVE: *Learner is to distinguish between a terminal behavioral objective and an instructional objective and know the two terms, so that he can identify terminal behavioral objectives and instructional objectives when presented with them and construct an example of each.*

Terminal Behavioral Objective. Terminal behavioral objectives are relatively specific statements of learning outcomes expressed from the learner's point-of-view and telling what the learner is to *do* at the end of instruction.

Examples of terminal behavioral objectives:
1. The learner is to identify the twelve cranial nerves so that he can, when given a diagram, label each nerve correctly.
2. The learner is to know the names of the fifty states so that he can list them (from memory) in any order.
3. The learner is to develop skill in typing so that he can copy a "rough" of a business letter of approximately 300 words, in proper style, within six minutes, and with no more than three errors.
4. The learner is to develop an understanding of social problems and conceptualize solutions so that he can:
   a. Define in writing a problem he has personally observed
   b. Describe in writing the problem in (a) above in terms of interpersonal relationships
   c. Outline the steps of a plan for solving that problem.

Terminal behavioral objectives are:
1. specific rather than broad
2. always expressed from the learner's point-of-view

5

3. statements which include a description of the behaviors of the learner or what he is able to do as a result of or at the end of instruction.

Terminal behavior. Terminal behaviors are specific descriptions of what learners are to *do* at the end of instruction. For all practical purposes *terminal behaviors* and *terminal behavioral objectives* are one and the same and will be so treated in this text.

What is the difference between a *terminal behavioral objective* and a *terminal behavior?* _____

Hopefully you replied **none,** or its equivalent, to this question.

Instructional objective. Instructional objectives are specific statements of intermediate learning outcomes necessary for acquiring a terminal behavioral objective, expressed from the learner's point-of-view and written in behavioral terms.

Instructional objectives are related to and necessary as behaviors in order to acquire a terminal behavioral objective. Instructional objectives can be thought of as intermediate behaviors to be acquired during the instructional period but not the final behavior toward which the learning is being oriented. They are intermediate in that they occur between the initiation of instruction and the learner's arrival at the desired terminal behavior. Generally they are logically and empirically derived, and thus necessary as acquired behaviors before the learner can obtain the terminal behavior. Sometimes they are called *enabling objectives.*

Examples of instructional objectives:
Terminal behavioral objective: Learner is to develop skill in solving equations of the type $H^+ R^- + R^+ OH^- \longrightarrow R^+ R^- + H^+ OH^-$ so that when given any four acids and any five hydroxides he can construct a balanced equation depicting the reaction.

Instructional objectives

A$_1$ Write a balanced equation
  A$_2$ Determine molecular equivalents in an equation
    A$_3$ Memorize the valences of common elements
      A$_4$ Memorize the formulas of common acids and common bases
        A$_5$ Conceptualize the model of acid + base = salt + water
          A$_6$ Conceptualize the concept of an equation
            A$_7$ Conceptualize the formula for an acid and a base

In this case the instruction approximates the sequence A$_7$-A$_6$-A$_5$-A$_4$-A$_3$-A$_2$-A$_1$-A, with A being the terminal behavioral objective and A$_7$—A$_1$ inclusive being instructional objectives.

Can You Tell the Difference?

At the end of each statement indicate "*T*" if you think it sounds like a *terminal behavioral objective* and "*I*" if you think it states an *instructional objective*:

1. The learner is to understand the relationship between mosquitoes, man, and malaria so that he can:
   a. list the types of malaria and the transmitting vector
   b. describe the life cycle of the causative agent of malaria
   c. write a description of the etiology of malaria.
2. The learner is to know the term "principal focus" and be able to use it correctly when discussing concave mirrors.
3. Student is to know the kinds of nouns so that when given a list of fifty he can classify them with no more than three errors within fifteen minutes.
4. Student is to use nouns skillfully so that he can compose twenty sentences without using any reference material and correctly underline all nouns used.

Check yourself here: 1 and 4 were "*T*" (terminal behavioral objectives); and 2 and 3 were "*I*" (instructional objectives). If you disagree you could be right, as some teachers may require students to know such things as illustrated in 2 and 3 and be able to perform accordingly at the end of instruction. However, 1 and 4 appear to be more important and possess greater transfer value than do 2 and 3, although these latter two may be attained during the learning process on the way to acquiring a more important terminal behavior as illustrated in 1 and 4.

In the following space write two terminal behavioral objectives and two instructional objectives.

Terminal behavioral objectives:

    1.

    2.

Instructional objectives:

    1.

    2.

Check yourself: In this case there is no right or wrong. Instead, the correctness of your choice depends on the perceptiveness of your viewpoint—whether the behavior is truly terminal (that which you want the learner to be able to do at the end of instruction)—or whether the behavior is one necessary to reach a higher or more complex terminal behavior, in which case it is instructional.

Criterion Test—Sections 2 and 3

Consider each statement and circle either **G**, **T**, or **I** if you think the statement represents a GOAL (**G**), a TERMINAL BEHAVIORAL OBJECTIVE (**T**), or an INSTRUCTIONAL OBJECTIVE (**I**).

1. Learner is to achieve competence in dealing with his peers.   G T I

2. Learner is to differentiate between goals, behavioral objectives, and instructional objectives so that he can classify them when given a list.   G T I

3. Learner is to develop skill in maintaining physical fitness.   G T I

4. Student is to learn to insert typing paper into the typewriter correctly.   G T I

5. Learner is to develop a vocational skill so that he or she can earn a living.   G T I

6. Student is to write a sample of each of three types of let- G T I
ters: thank you, application, and personal.

7. Pupil is to compose three different salutations for a person- G T I
al letter.

8. Pupil is to know the multiplication tables so he can recite G T I
to 9 times 9 correctly from memory.

9. Pupil is to develop skill in mathematics. G T I

10. Pupil is to solve correctly nine out of ten verbal problems G T I
in mathematics involving any one or combination of operations as adding, subtracting, multiplying, or dividing. G T I

11. Students at the end of the eighth grade are to develop G T I
skill in and an appreciation for a variety of ways of speech
making.

12. Learner is to match any ten of twelve given states and G T I
capitals from the total list of fifty pairs.

13. Student is to develop skill in map reading so that he can G T I
locate any of the twelve (12) geographic features (see
list).

14. Learner is to form the capital letters A through Z. G T I

Turn to the Appendix, A-1, page 97 for the answer key. Check
your test. You should score 12 or better. If you did not attain a score
of 12 or better you may wish to review sections 2 and 3, pages 3-8,
inclusive.

4

More About Objectives

TERMINAL BEHAVIORAL OBJECTIVE: Learner is to develop skill in writing objectives so that he can construct five examples without reference materials.

You have just read, in the prior sections, several terminal behavioral objectives and several instructional objectives. At this point you should know what they are, how they differ from goals, and be somewhat familiar with their structure.

Goals do have some use in constructing curricula or in lesson planning. Many educators have found that in developing terminal behavior objectives it is helpful to start with goals or at least broad statements of outcomes. Each broad statement (goal) is then broken down into smaller and smaller or more refined segments each of which then ends up as an objective.

Goals also may be useful in communicating with nonprofessional people and as summary statements of what schools are "all about." However, more effective communication, especially with students, depends upon stated objectives.

In summary, goals have three functions as above stated:

1. Serve as starting points for the development of objectives
2. Provide means of communicating with nonprofessionals
3. As statements summarizing the purposes of schools

We now turn to the structure of an objective (either terminal behavioral or instructional) and proceed with learning to express them in written form.

A properly expressed objective has three or four main features, though the fourth feature is not always present:

1. It is always expressed from the learner's point-of-view.
2. It is always specific.
3. It contains a behavioral description—a description of the behavior to be attained by the learner.
4. It contains a description of the special conditions, if any, under which the learner is to demonstrate his behavior.

Reread feature 1 above. Now choose either A or B (from each of the groups below) as the best statement of an objective which best conforms to feature 1:

1. A. To get the students to learn verbs so they can write ten sentences using ten given verbs correctly.
   B. Learner is to understand verbs so that he can write ten sentences using ten given verbs correctly.
2. A. To encourage pupils to appreciate good poetry.
   B. Pupils are to read at least two stories per week.
3. A. Students are to match words with their definitions.
   B. To acquaint the student with good dramatic literature.
4. A. Children are to develop poise and self-confidence.
   B. To allow the student to have an opportunity to discuss a vital subject.

Check yourself: Hopefully you said 1-B; 2-B; 3-A; and 4-A.

It is not difficult to express objectives from the student's viewpoint though many teachers fail to do it. If you don't, then the emphasis is in the wrong place. *Students* must do the learning—*not the teacher.*

Expressions like the following should be avoided. Each one listed here is taken from published objectives, showing how common the practice is of emphasizing the teaching behaviors when the important thing is the behavior of the learner.

Try not to use such phrases as:

To train the student —— ——
To aid the learner —— ——
To teach the student —— ——
To acquaint the student —— ——
To mold the student —— ——

To motivate the learner —— ——
To give the student —— ——
To instruct the debator —— ——
To inform the negative debator —— ——
To point out to students —— ——
To develop in the student —— ——
To bring about in the student —— ——
To produce in the learner —— ——
To encourage —— ——
To promote a —— ——
To integrate into the student's thinking —— ——
To convince the student —— ——
To aid in —— ——
To show importance of —— ——
To tell the children —— ——
To demonstrate to the student —— ——
To provide the student —— ——
To illustrate to the student —— ——
To convey to the student —— ——
To assist the student —— ——
To help the student to become —— ——
To afford the student the opportunity —— ——
To allow the student to have —— ——
To orient the student concerning —— ——
To instill in the student —— ——

These expressions emphasize what the teacher is doing rather than what the learner should be doing if he has learned. Learning is change in behavior, but it is each individual student who must change his behavior. It is possible to have a wide variety and a large number of teacher behaviors, yet have no learning—no change in student behavior.

———————

Vagueness is a common fault, as observation proves, when one examines a large number of the printed objectives available for guiding teachers and students. In fact many objectives are so vague as to be almost meaningless.

It is obvious that students go to school to learn—to learn what? To give answers to the *what* is to pin down and be specific about that which is expected of students. Vague expressions, which the reader or listener can interpret in many ways, do not communicate exactly what is to be learned or what the learner is to do at the completion of his learning. Vague, broad, ambiguous expressions in stating objectives do not aid the teacher in: (1) Selecting teaching materials, (2) Deciding on the proper methods to use, (3) Providing criteria proving that the student has achieved, or (4) Creating lesson plans.

Here are some typical objectives from recently published educational materials. Let's see what you think of them.

Objective: The students are to gain an understanding of the life of a certain economic group of people.

Think about what that objective says. What is meant by "understanding"? What about the life? What group of people? It is obvious that this objective communicates very little to the reader. It is too broad—too vague.

Objective: The student is to become acquainted with good dramatic literature.

What is meant by the term "acquainted with"? What is the student doing who is becoming "acquainted with"? What specific, dramatic, literary selections are being studied? Does this objective communicate exactly what is being studied, what is being learned, what the student is doing? Could you, as a teacher effectively plan a lesson or lessons around this objective? If two or more teachers read this objective would their interpretation of it be the same?

Objective: The student is to be informed of leadership responsibilities.

Consider this objective carefully. Could you, after reading it, select the exact learning materials needed, the visual aids you would need, the proper instructional activities the student should undertake, estimate the amount of time needed by the students to learn, and devise some type of evaluation which would prove the learner had successfully accomplished the objective? It is doubtful if you could do any of the above planning for instruction without knowing more specifically what the learner is to do. Objectives needn't be broad, vague, and ambiguous; on the contrary, they should be so expressed that the reader knows exactly what is to be learned. Even further, two or more readers should be able to interpret an objective without any serious disagreement as to the intent of that objective.

Let's consider three "pairs" of statements to be used in objectives and see if some expressions are not much more specific than others. For each pair choose either A or B as being the most *specific:*

1. A. Learner is to master the technical vocabulary.
   B. Learner is to be able to define in his own words the sixty-five terms in the *Glossary.*

2. A. Learner is to understand Spanish so that he can read orally an assigned paragraph and then correctly translate it into English.
   B. The learner is to develop an appreciation for Spanish and learn to read it.

3. A. Blindfolded, the learner is to be able to correctly assemble a 45-caliber, M 1919 pistol from the component parts which are in a field-stripped condition.
   B. The learner is to know all about hand guns and how to care for them.

Check yourself: I hope we agreed that in pair one it was B which was most specific. In pairs two and three it was A for each.

It is the specificity of objectives which makes them valuable to teachers in planning and evaluating instruction.

Thus far in section 4 of this text we have covered two character-istics of well-expressed objectives: (1) They are expressed from the learner's point-of-view, and (2) They are specific.

A third feature of an objective is that it contains a behavioral de-scription of what the learner is to be able to do after he has learned. Here is a demonstration of what we mean.

Objective A—(without behavioral description)
    The learner is to develop skill in using a spark plug gauge.
Objective B—(with behavioral description)
    The learner is to develop skill in using a spark plug gauge so that he can verbally describe the gap on each of six spark plugs.

It should be obvious that B is better than A as the expression of an objective because it tells specifically what the learner is to do—it contains a behavioral description. In B, the behavior is "verbally de-scribe" which, if he can do it correctly, certainly indicates that the learn-er has the proper skill in using the gauge.

There are hundreds of terms which indicate exact behaviors all of which can be learned in instructional settings. Such behaviors are the changes which we wish to have students acquire in the expression "Learning is *change* in behavior."

(Turn to Appendix B, page 102, for the presentation of an extended list of behaviors associated with nine classes of objectives.)

From the following paired expressions of objectives select either A or B (from each of the two groups below) as the objective which has a behavioral description.
    1. A. The learner is to understand the meaning of the term distilla-tion and develop skill in distilling water.

    B. The learner is to understand the causes of the Civil War (as presented in class) and be able to write a summary of the causes.

2. A. Students are to know compound subjects and their related verbs.
    B. Learners are to understand compound subjects and their related verbs so that when given twenty sentences with blanks they can supply the missing verbs.

You should have selected B as better than A, in each group. In 1-A, "to understand" and "to develop skill" are general terms naming classes of behaviors, and are not verbs which indicate a specific behavior. In 1-B, "write a summary" is a behavior you can observe.

If you had trouble with this one, don't be discouraged. A simple suggestion is: *close your eyes* and try to *visualize* what the student is *doing*. If the expression of the objective does not conjure a *doing* picture with your eyes closed then the objective does not have an observable behavior.

By these same tokens you should agree that 2-B is an exact expression of an observable behavior—"filling in blanks." In 2-A—"to know"—does not describe a behavior.

Let's try one more pair—one that will be more difficult.

    A. The student is to develop an understanding of usage of collective nouns so that he can use those nouns with appropriate verbs.

    B. The student is to develop an understanding of usage of collective nouns so that he can compose ten sentences in writing using those nouns with appropriate verbs.

We are in a rut. B is correct again. Actually there is a little difference in wording between A and B. Yet, in B, the wording "compose ten sentences in writing" is a definite, observable behavior that means the same thing to all readers.

In A of this pair, the expression "use" is open to interpretation—different readers would visualize many different behaviors which could indicate an ability to use.

We have to this point in section 4 covered three desirable features of an objective:

1. It is expressed from the learner's point-of-view.
2. It is specific—not broad and general.
3. It contains a behavioral description.

A fourth feature frequently found in objectives is a statement of *special conditions* under which the learned behavior is to operate. Not all objectives have special conditions—some do.

What are special conditions? They can be such elements as (a) time; (b) standards of performance; (c) aids; (d) restrictions.

Let's see how each of these might work.

    a. time:

- Learners are to develop knowledge of punctuation marks so that they can locate and identify by name all punctuation used, *within 15 minutes,* in a 300 word paragraph.

    b. standards of performance:

- Learners are to develop skill in using conjunctions so that they can fill in all the blanks in twenty sentences with conjunctions *with no more than two errors.*

- Learners are to develop skill in balancing oxidation-reduction equations so that they can supply the coefficients for each component in 20 equations *with 95% accuracy.*

    c. aids:

- Learners are to develop skill in machine lathe operations so that they can turn out a plumb bob from an *8" length of 2" diameter circular bar stock, using a 12" steel rule, a micrometer caliper, a set of 6" inside calipers, a set of 6" outside calipers, and a 3/4" steel bit,* to the specifications in manual 2.

- *Given a dictionary,* learners are to develop skill in expressing the meaning of terms in their own words so that they can write the meanings of twenty terms without error.

    d. restrictions:

- Learners are to understand the 60 technical terms found in the glossary so that they can use each term correctly in a sentence (oral or written) *without the use of a dictionary.*

———————————————

Try your skill in locating that part of an objective which contains a statement of a special condition; either time, standard of performance, an aid, or a restriction.

In each objective below, underline the words describing the special condition and then in the blank space following each objective classify the condition as to whether it was time, standard, aid, or restriction. First, here is an example:

1. The learner is to demonstrate skill in adjusting 20 set screws on the K-101-3 machine so that, when tested, each screw is adjusted properly *within ±.001 cm.*   1. standard

Now try your skill on the following eight objectives:

1. The learner is to gain an understanding of mineral identification so that he can orally name twelve of fifteen specimens as selected by the instructor from the forty-five studied in class.

1. _____

2. Within thirty minutes the learner is to demonstrate his understanding of letters of application and typing skill by composing and typing a finished letter of application to any hypothetical company.

        2. _____

3. The student is to know how to spell so that he can, from memory, write the correct spelling of the dictated words.

        3. _____

4. Blindfolded, the learner is to be able to correctly assemble a 45-caliber, M 1919 pistol from the component parts presented in field-stripped condition.

        4. _____

5. Using any source material of his choosing, the learner is to demonstrate understanding and skill in solving twelve word problems in statistics by recording the correct answer to each problem.

        5. _____

6. Students are to develop skill in locating geographic points when given latitude and longitude readings. For each pair of coordinates, the student will write a descriptive name of the point located. Students may use any maps or globes available to them in the classroom.

        6. _____

7. Learners are to spell with 95 percent accuracy, the dictated words in each spelling lesson.

        7. _____

8. The learner is to acquire skill in determining the degree of a monomial, so that he can write the degree of ten monomials within four minutes.

        8. _____

Time for checking yourself. Compare your underlined words and classification with the intended correct answers which follow.

1.	*twelve of fifteen*	1.	standard
2.	*within thirty minutes*	2.	time
3.	*from memory*	3.	restriction
4.	*blindfolded*	4.	restriction
5.	*any source material*	5.	aid
6.	*any maps or globes*	6.	aid
7.	*with 95 percent accuracy*	7.	standard
8.	*within four minutes*	8.	time

Some objectives have combinations of special conditions. Here are two examples:

1. Given a sheet of paper, protractor, map, and coordinate scale as provided, the student is to demonstrate within thirty minutes, his understanding of and skill in reading a map by:
   a. Identifying the object at 25.35-76.62.
   b. Determining the elevation to the nearest foot of the feature at 25.35-76.62.
   c. Answering Yes or No to this question. If you are 5′6″ tall and standing at point A (25.35-76.62) can you see point B (31.25-43.50)?
   d. State the gradient of the object indicated from point A (25.35-76.62) to point B (31.25-43.50).
   e. Determine the grid azimuth and back azimuth of a straight line drawn from point A (25.35-76.62) to point B (31.25-43.50).

2. The students are to develop skill in using nouns by composing twenty sentences from memory, each sentence containing two or more nouns, within forty-five minutes, and using a "word-picker" overwrite each noun with 98 percent accuracy.

In 1 (above) are two conditions: Given a sheet of paper (aid); within thirty minutes (time). In 2 (above) there are three conditions: from memory (restriction); within forty-five minutes (time); 98 percent accuracy (standard).

By now you should recognize a correctly expressed objective (either terminal behavioral objective or instructional objective) in written form. Each objective should meet these criteria:

1. Be expressed from the learner's point-of-view
2. Be specific
3. Contain a description of what the learner can do after he has learned—and it may possibly contain
4. A statement of some special condition as time, standard of performance, aids, or restrictions.

If you can pass this next check point you should also be ready to start writing objectives. In the following list of ten objectives there are some which conform to the first three criteria as outlined above, and some which do not. For each written objective circle *Yes* if it conforms to the specifications and *No* if it does not. If you choose No, then also circle one or more of the numbers 1, 2, or 3 (see below), so indicating the criterion being violated.

1. not expressed from learner's point-of-view
2. not specific
3. does not contain a description of what the learner is to do after he has learned.

Here are two examples of how it should be done.

1. The learners are to know the fifty states and their capitals so that they can draw a line from each state in list A to the proper name of the capitol of that state in list B. 1. (Yes) No   1 2 3

2. To develop in the student the ability to diagram sentences so that they can, when given ten sentences, diagram nine of them correctly.

 2. Yes (No) (1) 2 3

Example 1 was correct, so *Yes* was circled. Example 2 was deficient, so *No* was circled. It was not expressed from learner's viewpoint, so 1 was also circled.

Self Check Test—Section 4

For each of the ten objectives listed, circle *Yes* if the objective conforms to the specifications and *No* if it does not.

Further, if you circle *No*, then also circle one or more of the numbers *1*, *2*, or *3*, so indicating which of the three following criteria is being violated: (1) Expressed from the learner's point-of-view; (2) Specific, not general; (3) Contains a behavioral description.

1. Learners are to develop skill in reading so that they can read for one half hour.
 1. Yes No   1 2 3

2. Students are to gain skill in writing through practice.
 2. Yes No   1 2 3

3. Pupils are to understand, through reading, how water and dissolved molecules as $NaCl$, Na_2CO_3, $Ca(OH)_2$, and $CaSO_4$ pass through animal cell membranes.
 3. Yes No   1 2 3

4. Using a developing kit, 35-mm tungsten film, film laboratory, and Nikon camera fitted with 50-mm lens, as provided, each student is to load the camera, expose the film, unload the camera, develop the film, and dry it properly.
 4. Yes No   1 2 3

5. To develop in the student the ability to discriminate between color value and hue so that he can, using the chart handed out in class, verbally explain the difference between the two.
 5. Yes No   1 2 3

6. Learner is to develop the ability to analyze case history records so that he can prepare a written report on Form 22A, applying the principles learned in class.
 6. Yes No   1 2 3

7. To give the student an opportunity to learn how to multiply.
 7. Yes No   1 2 3

8. Learner is to know the twelve cranial nerves so that he can label them when given an outline drawing.

                    8. Yes No 1 2 3

9. To show the importance of diet in health so that each student can write a paragraph about it.
                    9. Yes No 1 2 3

10. Pupils are to develop skill in using a miter box so that when given four lengths of 1/2" x 2' cut stock they can, using the proper tools, construct an 18" x 22" mitered picture frame.

                    10. Yes No 1 2 3

Turn to the appendix, A-2, page 97 for the answer key. Check your own test. If you made over three errors you should reread section 4.

At this point it is important to call your attention to a small yet very important detail—the difference between the expressions *specific behavioral objective* and a *specific, behavioral objective*. The comma makes the big difference but let's explain so this distinction is not left to chance.

Some critics of behavioral objectives make a big point of the fact that objectives are too specific, too mechanical, too detailed, or too much like "having pupils dance on a string as puppets." Now it might be a valid argument that this is so if all we expected of students and *all students* is a specific behavior. However, this is not so. We want the objective to be *specific,* and *call for a behavior* rather than always calling for a *specific behavior!* Sometimes a specific behavior is expected. Let's try to illustrate. If I were asking the question, "What is two plus two?" I would expect all learners to come up with the specific behavior (answer) of four. At times objectives may call for specific behaviors but they may also call for varied behaviors which are specific. If I said to a group of learners, "Draw up a ten-point plan for making a trip," then I think I'm being specific and I want a behavior but not a specific behavior. In this case, the learner's responses could and should vary. Now, whether you write objectives calling for *specific behaviors* (all learners have the same response) or calling for a *behavior which is specific but varied* depends on the situation and the writer. In this text we will use illustrations of both types and hit this point again under the concepts of *open* and *closed* objectives; see section 8, page 57.

Criterion Test—Section 4

Write five Terminal Behavioral Objectives, using any subject matter or grade level of your choice. You are not to use any reference material.

There is obviously no standard answer for this Criterion Test. If you are satisfied that your objectives are expressed from the learner's point-of-view, that they are specific rather than general, and that each demands a behavior, then you are proceeding properly.

5

What Kind of an Objective Do I Have?

TERMINAL BEHAVIORAL OBJECTIVE: Learner is to understand a simplified taxonomy of objectives so that he can name the 9 classes and classify written objectives accordingly.

What is a taxonomy? It is a scheme for classifying a group of entities—in this case objectives. Bloom[2] and Krathwahl[3] have published the most comprehensive taxonomies of educational objectives to date. Their classifications however are complex and difficult for some people to work with. If you desire to do so, you may use their scheme.

An alternative taxonomy has been developed that is simpler and will be presented here.

First, there are three broad categories of objectives:

    A. Cognitive

    B. Affective

    C. Psychomotor

The *cognitive domain* includes those objectives that are most familiar to teachers as content of subjects and processes. Included are factual knowledge, understandings, processes, and strategies. These objectives are closely related to what we mean by "subject matter" and "thinking"—they are highly intellectual in nature.

The *affective domain* includes those objectives that are related to our emotional nature. Included are attitudes, appreciations, and interests.

---

2. B. S. Bloom, ed. *et al.*, *Taxonomy of Educational Objectives: Cognitive Domain* (New York: David McKay Co., Inc., 1956).
3. D. R. Krathwahl *et al.*, *Taxonomy of Educational Objectives: Affective Domain* (New York: David McKay Co., Inc., 1964).

The *psychomotor domain* includes those objectives that deal with body movements as motor sets and skills. Included are movements or actions without objects or tools, and movements or actions with objects and tools.

An outline summary of the complete taxonomy is presented below:

A. COGNITIVE DOMAIN
    Type I—Content area
        Class 1. K's —— Knowledges
        Class 2. U's —— Understandings
    Type II—Process area
        Class 3. P's —— Processes
    Type III—Problem solving area
        Class 4 S's — Strategies

B. AFFECTIVE DOMAIN
    Type IV—Emotional area
        Class 5. At's —— Attitudes
        Class 6. Ap's —— Appreciations
        Class 7. In's —— Interests

C. PSYCHOMOTOR DOMAIN
    Type V—Motor area
        Class 8. M's —— Movements without objects or tools
        Class 9. MO's —— Movements with objects or tools

All learning products can be classified into one of the nine classes outlined above. Let us now discuss each domain separately. Consider first then the COGNITIVE DOMAIN, with three types of objectives that contain four classes. The first of these objective types covers the area of content, containing two of the classes, as follows:

Class 1. K's—Knowledges. Knowledges are facts, names, dates, events, parts, low order concepts, low order associations; or in general, *information.*

Class 2. U's—Understandings. Understandings are comprehensions or apprehensions of general relations to particulars in high order events, the conversion of experience to intelligibility by bringing perceived particulars under appropriate higher order concepts, or the ability to use ideas in functional settings.

Knowledges are simple, low level, facts while understandings are higher order concepts, laws, generalizations, complex relationships. Generally speaking, *understandings* are more important as objectives than are knowledges although there can be no understanding without knowledge.

Which of these, A or B, is a *knowledge* objective and which is an *understanding?*

A. Learners are to be able to name the parts of a flower by labeling an outline diagram of a typical flower.
B. Learners are to illustrate the general reaction represented at A + B = Salt + H_2O by writing three balanced equations in symbolic notation, each with a different A reactant, and then in summary express the general rule verbally.

It should be fairly obvious that A is a knowledge and B an understanding objective.

It should be said in passing that many teachers have too many knowledge objectives as terminal behaviors. Although knowing names, dates, places, parts, and similar facts is sometimes important and necessary, facts are not the end of learning. Knowledges are often listed as instructional objectives but should be used sparingly as terminal behavioral objectives.

In writing objectives, it helps to classify them by incorporating the name of the class in the statement of the objective. Using the two objectives illustrated above, let's rewrite A using the term *know* or *knowledge:*

A. Learners are to *know* the parts of a flower so that they can name them by labeling an outline drawing of a typical flower.

When the class term is used in the objective (in this case, *know*) then the reader of the objective does not have to guess as to the class of objective intended.

Applying the rewriting to B, which was an understanding, we would have:

B. Learners are to *understand* the general reaction of acids and bases so that they can illustrate the general reaction represented by A + B = Salt + H_2O by writing three balanced equations in symbolic notation, each with a different A reactant, and then in summary express the general rule verbally.

Up to this point in section 5 we have explained K's (knowledges) and U's (undestandings). Both are frequently found in subject matter content. K's, though frequently listed as instructional objectives, are generally less important as terminal behavioral objectives than U's. In writing objectives, it helps to use the term of the class of objective intended.

Also in the COGNITIVE DOMAIN (see outline, page 23) are P's—*Processes*, considered under Type II objectives and grouped into class 3, and S's—*Strategies*, grouped under Type III objectives, in class 4, dealing with the area of problem solving. These two classes of objectives, considered fully below, are extensively involved whenever one thinks or solves problems. Processes and strategies are far from completely understood—our understanding of how people think and solve problems needs much further research and study.

Class 3. P's—Processes. Processes are specific mental skills which are any of a set of actions, changes, treatments, or transformations of knowledges, understandings, attitudes, appreciations, and interests generally used in a strategy in a special order to achieve the solution of a problem associated with the learning act, the use of learning products, or the communication of things learned.

The idea of processes is quite difficult for educators to grasp since it is new and most of us are uninformed as to what they are and how they work. Increasingly we have come to the realization that factual information (knowledge class of objectives) is not the sole end product of learning. Furthermore, in this day and age, knowledge is increasing so rapidly and the total is so vast, that no one can begin to "absorb" even a tiny fraction of it. As a consequence, soul searching has led teachers and others to find new approaches to what it means "to get an education." One approach is to concern ourselves less with knowledges as content and to concentrate more on *how people learn, how people think,* and *how people solve problems.* In short, many teachers are more concerned now with teaching thinking skills and problem-solving skills than they are with the minute data contained in texts and other resource materials. Facts and information are still important—in actuality, we can't think and solve problems without information. The difference in learning comes from the fact that learners are not now being required to memorize information for the sake of information itself. Instead, learners are being taught to *use* facts in thinking and problem solving. This approach is the *process* approach to education. Processes are the thinking skills or skills we use in collecting data, organizing data, transforming data, forming generalizations about data, formulating laws which govern data, theorizing when data is incomplete, inferring from a given set of data, etc.

Processes are those things we do (largely mental) as we abstract, analyze, associate, classify, conceptualize, create, etc. Processes are extremely important in learning and need more direct attention in classroom instruction. Exactly how many separate processes there are is not known. However, the following list of sixteen will cover the area well:

1.	Abstracting	9.	Evaluating
2.	Analyzing	10.	Generalizing
3.	Associating	11.	Measuring
4.	Classifying	12.	Perceiving
5.	Conceptualizing	13.	Predicting
6.	Creating	14.	Remembering
7.	Discriminating	15.	Synthesizing
8.	Estimating	16.	Translating

Here are two examples of process objectives. Notice we use the name of the process in writing the objective.

Example 1. The learner is to develop skill in *classifying* objects into sets of wood, glass, plastic, metal, leather, and clay so that when given thirty assorted objects he can group them properly into sets.

Example 2. Learner is to develop skill in *perceiving* so that when given thirty assorted objects which vary in weight and volume he can name the 2 varying factors and arrange the objects into weight sets and volume sets.

The last type and class of objectives in the COGNITIVE DOMAIN are Type III objectives known as S's—Strategies. S's are all grouped into Class 4. S's are heuristic entities or methods which result from either the art or skill utilized in devising or employing specific processes (refer to list above) as a plan in a special order to achieve a definable goal; usually the solution to a problem associated with the learning act, using learning products, or communicating about things learned.

More simply *strategies* or S's are plans or groups of skills used in problem solving. Let's illustrate a strategy in a hypothetical problem-solving situation—in this instance there are twelve major steps involving eight different processes. Strategies utilize processes.

Illustration of a strategy (process terms are in bold type):

Perceive a problem

  Generalize the perception

    Translate perceptions into definition or statement of problem

Collect data
Associate different bits of data
Measure various variables
Classify data
Estimate some factors
Generalize data
Conceptualize a hypothesis
Evaluate or test the hypothesis
Generalize or conclude

Strategies are not too difficult to comprehend—their name derives from the fact that they are "skillful plans" for problem solving. In "life after school" that is really what one attempts to do—"skillfully solve his problems." Learners need to think (use processes) in school about all kinds of problems and then proceed to solve them in an orderly, planned fashion. The plans or routes to problem solving are called *strategies*.

Most strategies are learned automatically as students solve problems. That is, learners in problem-solving situations discover for themselves the techniques, skills, or processes that work for them, as individuals. They also learn the processes necessary for a particular problem. Therefore, strategies develop uniquely—they are individualized or unique to the learner and unique to the problem. An infinite number of strategies are used by learners in problem solving.

Since strategies are for the most part automatically learned in problem solving situations they do not have to be specifically taught (learned) as separate entities. Therefore, strategies are infrequently expressed as objectives although they are learned in school.

There are some exceptions and these are generally referred to as *formal strategies*. A formal strategy is learned, for its own sake, because it is the one and only way to solve the problem in question; or for practical reasons it is the one and best way to solve the problem considering the grade and achievement level in question. In some subjects, as mathematics, we may teach a *solution* to a particular type of problem even though there may be more than one way to solve it. In this case we would be trying to get the learner to acquire a strategy. An example would be teaching pupils the step-by-step strategy to extract the square root of a number by the long method.

We have now covered the COGNITIVE DOMAIN. Recall the Types and Classes:

Type I	Type II	Type III
Class 1 — K's	Class 3 — P's	Class 4 — S's
Class 2 — U's		

Self Check Test

In the spaces below write the names of each of the four classes of objectives in the COGNITIVE DOMAIN and describe each one briefly in your own words.

1. _____

2. _____

3. _____

4. _____

Turn to Appendix, A-3, pp. 97-98, for answers to your self-check test.

The next area of objectives lies in the AFFECTIVE DOMAIN, in which are the three classes of Type IV objectives dealing with the human traits associated with emotion and feeling.

Of the three classes, the first is Class 5. Attitudes—At's. Attitudes are moods, convictions, or persistent dispositions to act in a given manner toward a person, thing, or event.

At's are difficult to express, especially in behavioral terms. Attitudes, such as acceptance of an idea, acceptance of another person, rejection of a way of life, tolerance of the opinion of others, etc. are hard to reduce to *what is the person doing* when he is accepting, rejecting, or tolerating. Most of what one feels is *covert*, while in writing an objective what you are seeking is an *overt* behavior that is "associated with" or "stands for" the covert behavior.

One problem in identifying overt behaviors which indicate attitudes is that different people react in different ways to the same inner feeling. A smile on Joe may be "pleasurable acceptance" while on Pete it may be "masked dislike" or "rejection." Another problem is acceptance by authority—the overt behavior acceptable to you as indicating possession of a given attitude may not be acceptable to some other authority.

All this is not saying that it is impossible to define behaviors for attitudes but it is difficult and may be relatively impossible in some instances. Until more research is completed on attitudes you must get along as best you can. Returning to our *acceptance-rejection* illustration we might suggest possible associated behaviors as:

1. Presence or absence of verbal expressions (oral or written) made by a person about another person, idea, or thing

2. Content of remarks as in 1 (above)

3. Scores obtained from attitude scales
4. Degree to which one relates to another—i.e. the degree of socialization or association with a person, idea, or thing
5. Use or nonuse of—as with accepting or rejecting an idea
6. Number of times (frequency) a person makes reference to a person, idea, or thing
7. A verbal defense of a position or idea
8. A verbal defense of another person's idea
9. Ratings by one or more observers

You are not expected to agree or disagree with this list. Perhaps you have ideas about behaviors other than those mentioned, which would make such behaviors equally or more acceptable to you as secondary, overt behaviors—thus indicating acceptance or rejection. The above list was presented at this point to illustrate it is possible to indicate some behaviors associated with attitudes.

The second of the three classes of behaviors in the AFFECTIVE DOMAIN also deals with feelings and emotions, referred to in the outline summary on page 23 as Class 6. Appreciations—Ap's. An Ap is a sensitive awareness or perception of the worth of an object or event, or the recognition of the aesthetic value of an object or event.

Worth, in this case, signifies far more than monetary value. Worth can be judged in terms of usefulness to a person, social utility, vocational utility, beautiful, pleasing, of historical significance or value, of scientific worth or value, recognizing that the entity under consideration has a part or role to play in (applicability), or is important enough to be considered (worthy of consideration).

A person can appreciate such things as:
1. a beautiful sunset
2. the contribution of an inventor
3. the hospitality extended by a friend
4. the role of science in modern life
5. the opportunity for an education
6. being motivated by a teacher

From these examples it should be obvious that, as with attitudes, appreciations are:

1. difficult to define
2. difficult to express in behavioral terms
3. sometimes even impossible to express in behavioral terms

4. more covert than overt
5. associated in many different ways with overt behaviors

Applying the same techniques to writing appreciations as to writing attitudes, the thing to do is *do* the best you can.

Here are some examples of overt actions or behaviors that indicate the presence of *appreciations:*

1. Expressed comments concerning values
2. Knowledge of components of value systems
3. Expressed critiques of specific entities, as works of art, etc.
4. Degree of consistency between personal value ratings and those of experts
5. Understanding of values as indicated by a person's ability to express comparisons of values as between a given A and B
6. Acquiring or possessing actual objects or examples of objects, as owning works of art
7. Frequency of or effort made to personally associate with; as in visiting an art museum, visiting a national monument, etc.

The third class of behaviors in the AFFECTIVE DOMAIN has to do with *interests*, and is referred to in the outline as Class 7. Interests—In's. In's are expressed desires or feelings which accompany special attention to objects or events or the readiness to attend to or be moved by objects or events.

Like attitudes and appreciations, interests are hard to define and pin down in behavioral terms. Also, like the others, interests are often more covert than overt. There are obviously behaviors associated with interests, so again, in expressing interest objectives the thing to do is *do* the best you can.

Here are some examples of overt actions or behaviors that indicate the presence of *interests.*

1. Scores obtained from interest inventories
2. Expressed desires (likes/dislikes)
3. Voluntarily attending to or participating in given X or Y
4. Number of times a person participates in an activity
5. Amount of time spent attending to a given activity
6. Degree to which a person becomes actively involved in or with an activity

In summary, the AFFECTIVE DOMAIN has one type of objective (Type IV) that contains three classes, each dealing with the feeling or emotional nature of man: Class 5, Attitudes or At's; Class 6, Appreciations or Ap's; and Class 7, Interests or In's. All objectives for these three classes are difficult, but not impossible, to express in behavioral terms.

(Note: Section 6 deals more extensively with AFFECTIVE BEHAVIORS.)

Self Check Test

I. In the spaces below write the names of each of the three classes of objectives in the AFFECTIVE DOMAIN and describe each one briefly in your own words.

1. _____

2. _____

3. _____

II. Names the four classes of objectives in the Cognitive Domain.

1. _____

2. _____

3. _____

4. _____

Turn to Appendix A-4, page 98 for answers to your self-check test.

The third and last major Domain is the Psychomotor Domain — that which contains motor sets and skills. This domain is easy to remember — it contains two classes of Type V objectives covering the motor area of which the first is Class 8, Movements without objects or tools; and Class 9, Movements with objects or tools.

Class 8. Movements—M's. M's are movements of the body or physical actions without involvement of outside objects or tools such as running, jumping, bending, nodding, etc.

Class 9. Movements with Objects—MO's. MO's are movements of the body with objects or tools such as batting, dribbling a ball, hammering, playing a violin, writing, painting, etc.

Movements, both with and without objects, are easy to describe in behavioral terms as the principle involved is always tied directly to a clearly defined overt behavior. For example, skill in throwing a baseball is not evidenced by underlining T or F on a TF examination, writing an essay, memorizing rules or other extraneous behaviors. Throwing is throwing and that covers the whole action part of the objective.

Examples of Psychomotor Objectives:

Class 8.   Movements——M's.

Example 1.   Learner is to develop skill in running so that he can run 100 yards in 13 seconds.

Example 2.   Learner is to develop skill in performing push-ups so that he can do, in proper style, twenty consecutive push-ups without intermittent rest.

Class 9.   Movements with Objects——MO's.

Example 1.   Learner is to develop skill in freehand lettering so that using a brush of his choice and ink he can prepare an 8" x 10" cardboard sales sign with product name and price as given.

Example 2.   Pupils are to develop skill in pottery making so that using the clay of their choice and wheel they can cast a bowl or vase of their own design within 10" x 10" x 10" dimension limits and side wall thickness not to exceed 1/4".

In the three Domains there are five types and nine classes of objectives in the taxonomy we have just covered.

The *classes* are the most important thing to remember and perhaps it will help you to remember the numbers. 4 — 3 — 2! There are four classes in the COGNITIVE DOMAIN—three classes in the AFFECTIVE DOMAIN—two classes in the PSYCHOMOTOR DOMAIN.

A. COGNITIVE DOMAIN
    Class 1 K's
    Class 2 U's
    Class 3 P's   4
    Class 4 S's
B. AFFECTIVE DOMAIN
    Class 5 At's
    Class 6 Ap's   3
    Class 7 In's
C. PSYCHOMOTOR DOMAIN
    Class 8 M's   2
    Class 9 MO's

Criterion Test—Section 5

Part I. Outline the classification of objectives by Domain, Types, and Class; or, if you can't, at least list the nine classes of objectives.

Part II. For each behavior listed below (notice that these are not complete expressions of objectives) indicate by letter symbol or class name the class of objective you think is indicated. Look over the whole set first noting the different examples already filled in. Complete the blanks not filled in.

1. run 100 yards— *M— Movement*

2. type a letter— *Mo— Movement with tool*

3. list the cranial nerves— _____

4. read and critically analyze— _____

5. express in writing how he believes— _____

6. name the parts of the camera— *K— Knowledge*

7. compare verbally the philosophy of X with that of Y—

   U— Understanding

8. classify any of laboratory collection of mosquitoes—

   P— Process (classify)

9. formulate a hypothesis— _____

10. plays golf twice a week— _____

11. develop in writing a plan for— _____

12. list the steps for the solution of the problem— *S—Strategy*

13. edit the rough manuscript— _____

14. prove that X equals Y— _____

15. high jump 48"— _____

16. judge a dog show— *U— Understand or possibly Ap— Appreciation*

17. watches TV football each Saturday— _____

18. spell the five words— _____

19. verify using the criteria devised— _____

20. voluntarily purchased art objects— _____

Turn to Appendix A-5, pages 98-99 for answers to this Criterion Test. You should score at least 15 counting the ones already completed in print.

6

More About
Affective Behaviors

TERMINAL BEHAVIORAL OBJECTIVE: *Learner is to understand more about attitudes, appreciations, and interests, their role in education, their identification, and the means of enhancing their occurence, so that, when given the five steps for analyzing the affective problem area, he can explain the solution and reason for each step.*

Affective behaviors are the least well understood of all the types of objectives and therefore frequently the root of a great deal of trouble and concern to teachers, administrators, and others. The intent of this section is to help you think more clearly about attitudes, appreciations, and interests so that you can make appropriate decisions concerning them in relation to teaching-learning situations.

He Doesn't Behave as I Do.

What do we mean when we say, "My son has a poor attitude toward ——"; or, "These kids are going to have to 'shape up' or 'ship out'"; or, "In my day, children acted differently"; or, "——"; etc.? Generally we are saying that *they* (whoever they are) do not behave as we do. It is similar to the situation when we say, "She has a poor personality"; or, "Mary has a lousy personality"; or, "Helen has no personality." Helen has a definite personality, not *no personality*. We really mean that Helen does not have a personality like ours or one acceptable to us.

In diagnosing Helen's situation (and ours) we need to find out if Helen lacks something—is she deficient in some behavioral sense in that she cannot perform? Is Helen lacking in one or more specific behavioral skills? Frequently the answer is *no*. If the answer is no, how can we expect specific training in the development of that behavior to help? The answer is, *we can't*.

A further illustration may pinpoint the problem. Let's say Helen doesn't *laugh* enough or *smile* enough to suit us. Is this because Helen doesn't know how to laugh or smile? Probably not. To find out why Helen doesn't smile or laugh we will have to look further—we will need to make some assumption other than that she lacks the ability to laugh or smile,— some assumption other than that Helen needs a course in *Laughing and Smiling*. Many *attitude, appreciation,* and *interest* situations are similar to this illustration. The learners often already possess the knowledges, understandings, and skills requisite to behaving but the particular behavior desired may not be present due to other reasons. It is often more of a *motivation* or *lack of desire problem* than it is a behavior deficiency.

Let's look at another example, *think it through,* and see if we can't analyze what is happening and what to do about it.

Step 1. Verification of a problem situation. Principal Jones is convinced the majority of his teachers have a "poor attitude toward teaching." What basis do we have for believing Jones? We can make these observations:

1. Jones makes much, verbally, of the fact that his teachers have a poor attitude.
2. Jones is frequently "grousing" about his teachers.
3. Jones frequently "picks" at his teachers.
4. Jones has called us in for help.

Now, how can we help? Jones expects us to do something (anything) by way of training or retraining, probably through in-service meetings, which will develop the proper attitude.

Additionally, Jones's observations or comments can be checked by interviewing the teachers or observing them to verify Jones's statements.

We have completed *Step 1*. It is clear Jones has a problem, but not necessarily a training problem. So we get into the matter by taking

Step 2. Clarification of the desired behaviors. We ask Jones, "What do you consider to be a good attitude—the one you want your teachers to possess?" Jones isn't sure—he hems and haws. With further and detailed questioning we find out that:

1. Teachers are lazy — they merely sit and talk to students
2. Teachers don't volunteer for extra assignments
3. Teachers maintain incomplete records
4. Teachers don't follow all of the published rules
5. Teachers don't attend PTA meetings
6. Etc.

Let's assume we have elicited from Jones fifteen or twenty more or less specific complaints about his teachers. We still don't have a list of desired behaviors, but they are easy to list from the negative statements (complaints) furnished by Jones. We draw up a list and check with Jones to be sure that he would be happy if his teachers:

1. Lectured less — used more visual aids — etc.
2. Volunteered for sponsorship of extra-curricular organizations
3. Kept neat and up-to-date attendance records
4. Checked in by 8:00 A.M. daily
5. Attended PTA meetings
6. Etc.

Jones, after reading the list, smiles and says, "Yes, that would be great! I sure wish my teachers were like that. Can you teach them to do these things?"

Before we answer Jones we must take:

Step 3. Determination of performance deficiencies. We can't hasten to assure Jones that we can train his teachers until we are sure the problem is amenable to training remediation. Before we propose a course of *attitude instruction* we must find out certain things. We ask Jones:

1. Do your teachers have visuals available? Do they know how to use 8-mm films, slides, etc. (He says, "Yes.")
2. Do your teachers know how to volunteer? (He says, "Certainly they do.")
3. Do your teachers know how to keep attendance records? (He says, "Yes, of course.")
4. Do your teachers know how to tell time and how to go through the "check-in" procedure? (He says, "Don't be silly, of course they do.")
5. Do your teachers know how to go to PTA meetings? (He says, "Naturally they do.")
6. Etc.

It should be obvious to you, as it became to Jones, that his teachers already had the abilities and skills necessary to proper performance. Some other reason(s) were needed to explain the teachers' lack of appropriate behavior (proper attitude). Actually, attitudes, appreciations, and interests are not isolated abilities or skills in themselves, but as pointed out in section 5 they are habit patterns, awarenesses, and expressed feelings. Poor attitudes are rarely due to a lack of ability—there is rarely a performance deficiency.

Another way of saying this is: Poor attitude (lack of appreciation, low interest, etc.) is generally due to the absence of stimuli which elicit the desired behaviors, rather than a lack of skill or behavior ability. The person doesn't perform because he doesn't want to perform rather than that he doesn't know how to perform.

We still haven't found out why the teachers are behaving as they are rather than the way Mr. Jones desires. To help find the reasons you take:

Step 4. Identifying reasons for present behaviors, and conversely, reasons for absence of desired behaviors. We ask Mr. Jones in Step 4, why are the teachers merely lecturing and is there any incentive to use visuals? This identification procedure can take this form of double questioning:

1A. What are the results (rewards/punishments) of lecturing?
1B. What are the results (rewards/punishments) of *not* lecturing? (i.e., using visuals)
2A. What are the results (rewards/punishments) of volunteering for extracurricular events?
2B. What are the results (rewards/punishments) of *not* volunteering for extracurricular events?
3A. What are the results (rewards/punishments) for keeping good attendance records?
3B. What are the results (rewards/punishments) for *not* keeping good attendance records?
4A. }
4B. } Etc.

Jones replied that the school couldn't force teachers to not lecture, to volunteer, to attend PTA meetings, etc., and that in reality nothing happened if they failed to keep good records (poor records were better than none), if they failed to volunteer (he was just happy to get a few teachers involved), and that if they checked in after 8:00 A.M. (late) it was no disaster as long as it was before 8:30 A.M.

From this we are led to two conclusions:

1. In some cases the results (rewards/punishments) of not behaving like a good teacher are of little significance; and,
2. In some instances there is no incentive to be a good teacher.

The teachers did not have the correct attitude because the teaching environment did not expect or encourage correct attitudes. The conclusion is that the teachers had the correct behaviors (were capable of performing) but they did not exhibit these behaviors because there was no cause for so doing.

How then, do we get the teachers to exhibit correct behaviors—shape up to the correct attitude? This leads to:

Step 5. Listing of positive factors (non-aversive) which will be causative agents encouraging the exhibition of acceptable behaviors. In discussing Step 5 with Mr. Jones the following were identified as being possible incentive factors:

A. Personal relationships between administration and staff.
   * Smile from Jones
   * Compliments from Jones
   * Encouragement from Jones
   * Support from administration

B. Personal rewards to staff.
   * Time off for work well done
   * Preferential treatments in scheduling of classes as a result of correct behavior
   * Private office assignments
   * Augmentation of supplies and materials requests
   * Exclusion from distasteful tasks (i.e., noon and hall duty)
   * Permission to travel to professional meetings at school expense
   * Invitation to act as consultant expert
   * Favorable parking position in parking lot
   * Bonus pay schedule for extra curricular assignments
   * Appointment to positions of leadership
   * Selection of limited personnel to receive cash awards for excellence of service
   * Time released for research
   * Time released for writing
   * Awarding of master teaching awards (by way of yearly certificates)
   * Appointment to school policy council, meeting once a month for a free lunch
   * Reduced teaching load (classes)
   * Reduced teaching load (number of students)
   * Permission to develop special projects
   * Etc.

By the time Step 5 was completed Mr. Jones was more enlightened as to his problem. He began to see that the system was not structured nor administered to encourage good teaching, and that he, himself, was a part of that system.

To make a long story short, Mr. Jones with our help, concluded that he did not have an instructional (training problem); rather, there existed a *management systems* problem.

Reviewing the steps by which a person (or school) decides if they have a training problem in the affective area, and what to do about it, we have:

Step 1.   Verification of a problem situation.

   Solution: A judgment based on direct observation of the problem situation.

Step 2.   Clarification of the desired behaviors.

   Solution: Define what the possessor of the correct attitudes, appreciation, or interest is like (what he does, or even who he is, giving an example).

Step 3.   Determination of performance deficiencies.

   Solution: Determine performance deficiency by comparing the idealized performance (step 2) with the actual performance (step 1). You also discover and conclude whether the desired performance is an ability or skill already possessed by the person or persons with whom there is concern.

Step 4.   Identify reasons for present (actual) behavior, and conversely the reasons for the absence of desired behaviors.

   Solution: Ask these two questions: (1) What is the result (reward/punishment, of doing behavior X; (2) What is the result (reward/punishment) of not doing behavior X?

Step 5.   List the positive factors (non-aversive) which will be causative agents encouraging the exhibition of acceptable behaviors.

   Solution: List the factors (rewards, incentives, or situations) which will make people want to behave or encourage them to behave in the manner desired in step 2.

———————

The chart on page 44 should help you understand the five steps and what to do at each step. Review this chart several times until you are sure you can list the five steps and explain in your own words the function or reason for each one.

———————

There is a conclusion to the "Tale of Mr. Jones, Principal":

Don't assume that attitudes, appreciations, and interests can be taught directly. They are not in themselves abilities or skills. If an at-

titude depends on a skill the learner does not have, then the skill can be learned but the correct attitude does not necessarily follow.

If not skills, knowledges, or understandings then what are effective objectives? They are, as we've said before, feelings exhibited by persons in behavioral complexes, awarenesses, and habit patterns.

For example, POOR PERSONALITY may be:

Doing X	instead of	Doing Y
crying	" "	laughing
being silent	" "	talking
sitting down	" "	dancing
letting attention wander	" "	concentrating
	etc.	

However, the person considered to have a poor personality probably (undoubtedly) knows how to laugh, talk, dance, and attend. There must be other reasons (causes) for his/her behavior. These causes are more related to lack of motivation or desire than to lack of skill.

Here are several reasons why people have behaviors (poor attitude, lack of interest, no apparent appreciation) other than those you would like to see those persons possess (which are desirable or certainly more acceptable).

1. Their present behavior is more personally gratifying. *They don't want to change; their present behavior is rewarding.*
2. To change their behavior would require a lot of work or effort they don't perceive as worth expending. *It is not worth the effort to change; they foresee no reward in changing.*
3. To change would cost them something—they feel they would lose more than they would gain. *It would be punishing to change.*
4. The environment in which they operate restricts or prohibits change. *They feel it is impossible to change.*

Conclusion. *Most of the time correct attitudes, greater appreciation, and heightened interest are developed as behavioral patterns if the system (environment) in which the person operates rewards such behavioral patterns.*

Implications for the Classroom

What implications do we find for the classroom in all of this? Frankly, many learners do not demonstrate behaviors desired by teachers because:

S E Q U E N C E

Step 1. Locate and verify problem	Step 2. Clarify the desired behaviors	Step 3. Determine if the problem is a performance deficiency	Step 4. Identify reasons for presence or absence of the desired behavior and the actual behavior	Step 5. Listing of the factors which will cause persons to perform correctly

A C T I O N S

			(Ask both questions)	
1. Observe the problem situation.	List the behaviors desired or,	1. Compare the actual behavior with the desired behaviors.	1. What is the result (pay off) of performing correctly?	1. Make a list of all the positive factors (rewards, conditions, consequences) which will encourage the desired behavior.
2. Interview relevant personnel.	Locate an example of the desired behavior or,	2. Determine if the desired behaviors are within the repertoire of behaviors of those expected to perform.	2. What is the result (pay off) of not performing correctly?	2. Revise the system (environment) to include the appropriate factors in 1 (above).
3. Conduct a task analysis.	Describe an acceptable example of the desired behavior.	3. If the desired behaviors can be performed then training is not the solution.		
		4. If the desired behaviors cannot be performed then training might be a part of the solution.		

1. Their present behavior is more rewarding
2. Trying to behave in the desired way they find punishing
3. Peer pressure to behavior in a way different from what is desired is greater than any adult pressure which can be exerted
4. To change their behavior would cost them in time and energy—what they perceive as gain is not worth the effort
5. They perceive the classroom in which they operate far differently than the teacher viewing the same classroom. Their perception may be that the classroom, teacher or the school is restrictive or prohibitive
6. They are "bored to death"
7. They do not perceive any reward to themselves (relevancy) in that which is expected of them.

For the teacher, the implications are clear—you must manage the classroom setting and the curricular content so that learners perceive the worthwhileness of what they are learning. The learning must be rewarding, both in substance and in process.

You might answer these questions to yourself about the classrooms you operate. Hopefully you will say "yes" to each.

1. Are the children free to express themselves even if their opinions are quite different from the other learners and from mine?
2. Do I reward good behavior, or do I only punish poor or unacceptable behavior?
3. Do I make efforts to develop only relevant terminal behaviors?
4. Do the children perceive the importance of learning what I'm teaching?
5. Are prompt, neat, complete assignments rewarded?
6. Are the learners required to apply and use what they learn?
7. Do I make the learning as pleasant and enjoyable as I can?
8. Do I regularly analyze the classroom to see if any restrictions to learning exist and do I remove all restrictions possible?

Self Check Test

In the spaces following each of the five steps, briefly state, in your own words, the reason(s) for each step and how the step is carried out in practice.

Step 1. Location and verification of the problem

Step 2. Clarification of the desired behaviors

Step 3. Determination of performance deficiencies

Step 4. Identification of reasons for present behaviors, and conversely, the reasons for the absence of desired behaviors

Step 5. Listing of the positive factors which will be causative agents encouraging the exhibition of acceptable behaviors

---

Check yourself by reviewing the chart on page 44 and comparing your answers with comments under ACTIONS. If you did not get the steps correct, review the chart and try to determine the meaning and reasons for each step in relationship to the problem of identifying, clarifying and solving problems in the AFFECTIVE DOMAIN.

If you completed this Self Check Test successfully consider that you have successfully met the criteria of section 4. If you did not complete this Self Check Test successfully, then, after reviewing the chart on page 44 and/or the whole of section 6, take the Criterion Test which follows.

Criterion Test—Section 6

In the spaces following each of the five steps, state briefly, in your own words, the reason(s) for each step and how the step is carried out in practice.

Step 1. Location and verification of the problem

Step 2. Clarification of the desired behaviors

Step 3. Determination of performance deficiencies

Step 4. Identification of reasons for present behaviors, and conversely, the reasons for the absence of desired behaviors

Step 5. Listing of the positive factors which will be causative agents encouraging the exhibition of acceptable behaviors

---

Turn to the chart, page 44, and compare your responses with the comments under ACTIONS.

7

Covert and Overt Behaviors or Primary and Secondary Behaviors[4]

TERMINAL BEHAVIORAL OBJECTIVE: *Learner is to understand primary and secondary behaviors so that he can analyze behaviors in written objectives and gain skill in correctly expressing behaviors in objectives of his own creation.*

At this point you should be getting rather sophisticated in expressing objectives. There is another problem in writing objectives and it was alluded to in section 5 in the discussion concerning the AFFECTIVE DOMAIN. This is the problem of *covert* and *overt* behaviors relative to the intent of the objective.

Many objectives have a primary concern for a behavior that is covert. This would be true of such behaviors as perceiving, seeing, comparing, loving, hating, abstracting, generalizing, formulating, etc. In these cases, the objective must call for a secondary behavior which is overt—the assumption is that the secondary behavior which is associated with the primary behavior, can stand for the primary behavior, or is a natural result of the primary behavior.

Here is an example of what the problem is:

Terminal Behavioral Objective: Learner is to estimate volumes of liquids in assorted, irregular containers so that he can write the total volume, in fluid ounces or cubic centimeters, with error limit of one fluid ounce or 30 cc, for eight of ten given containers.

---

4. This problem is the topic of concern in the article by Robert F. Mager "Search for the Simple," *Illinois Journal of Education* 61, no. 2 (February, 1970).

What is the primary behavior requested in this objective? It is *estimating.* Is estimating a covert or overt behavior? It is *covert.* What is the secondary behavior requested? It is *writing.* Is it covert or overt? It is *overt.*

In this example, the creator of the objective intended for the learner to develop skill in estimating and the alert, capable teacher to design the instructional activities accordingly. The thrust of instruction would be aimed at estimating. Estimating, however, cannot be *seen!*

The creator of the objective either consciously or unconsciously (hopefully the former) realizing *you can't measure estimating directly by an estimating behavior* selected a secondary behavior which was to stand for or be an acceptable replacement for estimating.

At this point two problems arise. First, will the secondary behavior selected by the creator of the objective be an acceptable replacement as judged by others? That is, will the secondary behavior be judged a *valid* replacement for the primary behavior intended by the majority of educators using the objective? The second problem concerns the *appropriateness* of the secondary behavior—is the secondary behavior within the ability of the learner for the grade or level for which the objective is intended?

In our example we would probably answer "yes," to the question of validity. Most teachers would believe that the ability to *write estimated volumes* is an acceptable secondary replacement for the primary behavior of estimating volumes. To the question of appropriateness we would probably also reply "yes," as the ability to write the numbers would undoubtedly be within the repertoire of behaviors possessed by learners who were acquiring the estimating skill.

Now let's examine an objective where the secondary behavior could well be judged a poor choice.

Terminal Behavioral Objective: Learners are to know the differences between winter and summer in the northern hemisphere so that they can draw a picture of each season depicting the differences.

Analyzing this objective, the learners are to know the *differences.* Being a class 1.K objective it is low level, so we can assume the learner is to develop a low level ability to differentiate. Differentiating appears to be the covert, primary behavior called for. The overt behavior which is to stand for, or represent proof of the learner's ability to differentiate, is *draw a picture.* In relation to the two problems of validity and appropriateness it would appear that the secondary behavior is valid but not appropriate. That is, "drawing a picture of each season" is probably an acceptable way for a student to indicate he knows the differences between the seasons. Drawing pictures, in this case, is to do the job of indicating to the teacher that the student "knows the differences between the seasons" and undoubtedly the pictures would do the job effectively. However, this would only be the case if the students could *draw*. If drawing skill is not within the students' repertoire of behaviors, then the secondary behavior is not appropriate for the age and/or grade level. Learning the seasons is frequently a first grade concept. Very few first grade pupils have much skill in drawing. In this case the objective should be redesigned, incorporating a more appropriate secondary behavior.

A further complication is quite likely to result if the secondary behavior were to be unchanged as "draw a picture of each season." Since the ability of the learners at this age/grade level to "draw" is quite primitive and will evidence wide variability from learner to learner, the teacher will be inclined to evaluate (grade) the drawing (secondary behavior) rather than the learner's ability to *differentiate* (the primary behavior). This possibility defeats the whole purpose of the objective.

At this point, let's stop and critically analyze objectives. Please read each objective first and analyze it to the best of your ability before reading the analysis.

Terminal Behavioral Objective A:
> Learner is to know the parts of a flower and label a diagram provided by the instructor.

Please criticize this objective referring when necessary to the analysis listed below. By doing this you will learn how to analyze an objective.

Analysis of A:
1. It is expressed from student's point-of-view.
2. It is a class 1.K objective.
3. There is no primary behavior described. *Knowing* is not a behavior but the name of a class of behaviors.
4. The secondary behavior is *labeling*.
5. The secondary behavior is probably valid; but impossible to judge, in this case, without a primary behavior against which to judge it.
6. The secondary behavior is probably appropriate; that is, within the repertoire of behaviors of the learners who are expected to be learning the parts of a flower.
7. This is a poor objective and needs to be redesigned by including a primary behavior, as *to name*.

Terminal Behavioral Objective B:

> Learner is to understand how to assemble an M-1 rifle so that he can take it apart and put it together without any instructional aid.

Please analyze Objective B as we did A above *before* you read the analysis of B listed below. You make the analysis, then check your answer.

Analysis of B:

1. It is expressed from the student's point-of-view.
2. It is specific.
3. It is a class 2.U objective.
4. The primary behavior required is *assemble*.
5. The primary behavior is overt so a secondary behavior is not required.
6. The author of the objective confused the issue by also stating that the learner was to *disassemble* and *assemble*.
7. The requirement to disassemble is not valid unless the objective is rewritten asking the learner to understand "how to disassemble and assemble. . . ."
8. There are conditions (a restriction to the behavior expressed as "without any instructional aid").
9. This is a poor objective (see 6 and 7 above) and needs to be redesigned.

Terminal Behavioral Objective C:

> Learner is to develop skill in analyzing behavioral objectives so that when given poor examples he can, without guidance, rewrite the objectives to conform to acceptable standards as taught in class.

Please analyze Objective C above *before* you read the analysis listed for C below. You make the analysis, then check your answer.

Analysis of C:

1. It is expressed from the learner's point-of-view.
2. It is specific.
3. It is a class 3.P (analyze) objective.
4. *Analyze* is the primary behavior.
5. Analysis is covert, so a secondary overt behavior is required.
6. There is a secondary behavior required and it is *rewrite*.
7. The secondary behavior is probably valid. If the learner can rewrite an objective that has errors, and the new version is error free, it is a safe assumption that the learner "analyzed" the objective.
8. The secondary behavior, however, is probably not appropriate. Learners developing skill in analyzing objectives may not at that point of learning be able to write or rewrite objectives. Perhaps a more appropriate behavior to require as proof of the learner's ability to analyze would be to write his analysis as a list of statements.

9. The objective states learning conditions.
10. The objective is questionable (see 8 above) and may need redesigning.

Terminal Behavioral Objective D:

Learner is to devise and test a hypothesis concerning the relative achievement, after 9 months, of two classes of students, $N = 30$ in each, each learning chemistry by a different method; the methods being C - Control (assign, study, recite) and X - Experimental (self paced, laboratory instruction); the project to be written as a report which shall include: (1) statement of hypothesis, (2) description of method and materials, (3) summary of results, and (4) conclusions.

Please analyze Objective D, above, *before* you read the analysis of D, below.

Analysis of D:

1. It is expressed from the learner's point-of-view.
2. It is specific.
3. It is a class 4.S (strategy) objective.
4. *Devise* and *test* are the primary behaviors.
5. Devise and test are covert behaviors.
6. *Write* is the secondary, overt behavior.
7. The secondary behavior (writing a report) is *valid*, as it could not be done without completing the primary behavior (devise and test).
8. The secondary behavior is appropriate as learners at this level who are hypothesizing and testing can certainly write a report.
9. The objective states learning conditions.
10. The objective appears to be acceptable.

One more problem remains concerning primary and secondary behaviors. It may be that an objective calls for a primary behavior which is covert and no secondary behavior is mentioned. In this case the reader (consumer) of the objective is allowed to interpret the objective in his own way—a very inefficient and impractical state of affairs. Let's illustrate what we mean.

Terminal Behavioral Objective E:

Learner is to develop skill in solving verbal arithmetic problems so that he can correctly solve eight out of ten problems calling for operations involving adding, subtracting, multiplying, and dividing.

Please analyze Objective E, above, *before* you read the analysis of E, below.

Analysis of E:

1. It is expressed from the learner's point-of-view.
2. It is specific.
3. It is a class 2.U (understanding) and 4.S (strategy) objective.
4. *Solve* is the primary behavior.
5. Solve is a covert behavior.
6. There is no specific secondary behavior called for although "solve" implies one.
7. There is a standard.
8. This objective needs to be redesigned (see no. 6, above).

In this case, were the consumer of the objective a student, he or she could well assume that writing the answer was a correct secondary behavior, or the way to "solve," and behave accordingly. The teacher, on the other hand, may desire the answer plus the solution work and discount (grade lower) the student's behavior accordingly. We would have a communication failure because the objective does not clearly specify the secondary behavior which the teacher is willing to accept as taking the place of the primary behavior. The term *solve* should be "spelled out" to mean *write the solution,* or *show your method and the answer,* or any appropriate behavior you would be willing to accept as proof of "solving."

―――――――

You should be ready to take the criterion test for this section. Read the directions carefully.

―――――――

Criterion Test—Section 7

Part I.   In each objective there are verbs representing behaviors, either primary or secondary. In the proper space at the right fill in the blank with the behavioral term. The primary behavior may not always be listed first in the objective. See examples below.

Examples:

1. Learner is to know the characteristics of vertebrates so that he can list them in writing.
   1a. Primary behavior: *Characterize*.

   1b. Secondary behavior: *List*.
2. Learner is to understand the philosophy of Rousseau so that he can write (in an hour period) an essay summar-

izing Rousseau's thoughts and comments about government and education.

2a.   Primary behavior: *Summarizing*.

2b.   Secondary behavior: *Write*.

---

1.   Learners are to identify objects as to whether they are or were derived from living organisms so that when given twenty objects they can sort them into two categories, living and nonliving.

1a.   Primary behavior:_____.

1b.   Secondary behavior:_____.

2.   Learners are to contrast the features of editorial, report and news styles of writing.

2a.   Primary behavior:_____.

2b.   Secondary behavior:_____.

3.   Learners are to develop skill in plotting coordinates so that when given bivariable data on rectilinear semilogarithmic, logarithmic and polar coordinates from a table of values they can plot appropriately.

3a.   Primary behavior:_____.

3b.   Secondary behavior:_____.

4.   Learners are to develop skill in interpreting flow, organization and distribution charts so that they can verbally explain the function of and summarize any of a series of three prepared charts.

4a.   Primary behavior:_____.

4b.   Secondary behavior:_____.

5.   Learners are to determine the direction and magnitude of the resultant in a given coplanar system by the triangle method and plot the solution on graph paper.

5a.   Primary behavior:_____.

5b.   Secondary behavior:_____.

Part II.   For each of the five objectives above state whether the primary and secondary objectives were covert (C) or overt (O).

1a. _____ 2a. _____ 3a. _____ 4a. _____ 5a. _____
1b. _____ 2b. _____ 3b. _____ 4b. _____ 5b. _____

Part III. Write two objectives as follows:

1. An objective with an overt primary behavior in which no secondary behavior is needed.

2. An objective with a covert primary behavior and an overt secondary behavior.

Answers to Criterion Test — Section 7 in Appendix A-6, pp. 99-100.

8

What Is the Difference Between an Open and Closed Objective?

TERMINAL BEHAVIORAL OBJECTIVE: *Learner is to develop skill in analyzing objectives as to being open, closed, or part open and part closed so that he can, when given three objectives classify in writing each behavior as open or closed.*

Learner is to understand open and closed objectives so that he can create one written example of open, one of closed, and one open and closed objective.

In section 4, pages 10-20, we referred to the problem of open and closed objectives. The idea was introduced by differentiating between what was meant in this volume by a *specific behavioral objective* and a *specific, behavioral objective.* [Remember, the comma made the difference.]

By way of review, we indicated that a specific behavioral objective called for all learners to behave the same—the behavior called for was a specific behavior. On the other hand a specific, behavioral objective permitted each learner to make a response, such responses could vary from learner to learner, yet each response *would be specific.*

A specific behavioral objective is *closed* and a specific, behavioral objective is *open*. (The comma makes the difference.)

Examples of Closed Objectives:

1. Learner is to develop skill in adding so that when given any 50 of the 100 addition facts he can add (by recording the sums) 48 of them correctly within 6 minutes.

Assuming a class of twenty-five first grade pupils each of whom is "taking the test" (fifty addition fact problems), and at the end of the test we are to score the test, we would expect the same (exact) response from each pupil. If the exact response was not present (the correctly written sum) for each item, then that response (behavior) would be wrong.

2. Learner is to know and name the parts of a simple AC motor so that he can label a given outline drawing.

Again, each respondee would theoretically be responding exactly the same as every other learner. This is a *closed* behavior.

Examples of Open Objectives:

1. Learner is to develop skill in using resource and reference material so that he can construct a written, detailed outline plan for a twenty-one day trip into Mexico leaving from and returning to the city of Juarez.

In this case each of twenty-five learners would normally be expected to have a response different from the others, although each learner's response would be specific. When the objective allows each learner to perform differently—to demonstrate an original or self-designed response—that is an *open* behavior.

2. Learner is to develop an understanding of the relationship between industrial production and location so that he can:
   (a) Name two industries not now present in his community which could be there
   (b) For each industry in (a) above, list the natural resources needed, the required labor, and the required tools, and
   (c) Using a community map, locate the two industries and justify the location in writing.

Again, each learner would be responding specifically, yet each respondee would undoubtedly write a response different from every other learner's response.

Examples of Open and Closed Objectives:

1. Learner is to develop research analysis skills so that he can:
   (a) When given a topic, locate and name five sources pertaining to it
   (b) Using two of the sources in (a) above, list by page references items of information pertaining to the topic
   (c) Classify each reference in (b) above listing it as either primary or secondary
   (d) Write in his own words the definition of *subjective evidence* and *objective evidence*
   (e) List ten subtitles pertaining to the topic which could be explored in some type of index
   (f) List three indexes where the subtitles in (e) above could be found.

It would appear that behaviors (a)-(b)-(e)-(f) are open and (c)-(d) are closed. That is, the learner's responses to items (a), (b), (e), and (f) could be substantially different while in (c) and (d) their responses would be substantially alike or there is no learner "choice" as in (c). The source can't be both primary and secondary; one or the other is correct.

2. Learner is to develop an understanding of the concept of community responsibility (control and prevention) in relation to pollution so that he can:
   (a) List the five local agencies (private or public) which are involved in controlling or preventing pollution
   (b) List the ten sources of known pollution in the community and indicate whether they are controlled or uncontrolled
   (c) Describe in writing the ways and means open to any citizen wishing to help with the pollution problem.

It would appear that (a) and (b) are closed but that (c) is open. Students behaving as required in (a) and (b) must list *the five* and *the ten* while in (c) they can propose a variety of ways a citizen could contribute or help with the pollution problem.

Now let's see if we can apply the open and closed concept to two objectives.

Learner is to develop the ability to express ideas and relationships between ideas so that he can:

(a) When given twenty word groups mark them as complete sentences (CS) or less than a sentence (LS)

(b) For each (LS) in (a) above, complete the word group to form a complete sentence

(c) Using any three or four sentences (originally complete or completed by you) from (a) above form a paragraph

(d) Using any two sentences (originally complete or completed by you) form, by adding two or three more original sentences, a paragraph

(e) Construct an original paragraph which contains a topic sentence and in addition a minimum of one supporting sentence containing information, one sentence pertaining to a value judgment of the data, and one sentence containing a summary or conclusion.

Indicate, by placing a **C** for closed or an **O** for open, the type of each behavior, (a) through (e) above, that would be your response.

(a)＿＿＿＿＿   (d)＿＿＿＿＿

(b)＿＿＿＿＿   (e)＿＿＿＿＿

(c)＿＿＿＿＿

I marked them all **O** except (a) and (b). In (a) word groups are either sentences or they are not. Each learner's response is expected to be like every other learner's response. In (b), even if we admit that each learner's choice of words might be different, there is very little leeway for originality or a self-designed response. [You just might have rated (b) as **O** or open because the learner did add words of his own. If you reasoned this way, then you are right. In this example, (b) is hard to specify as being conclusively **C** or **O**. I still judge it more closed than open.]

Let's try another.

Terminal Behavioral Objective:

Learner is to perceive characterization in novels or short stories so that he can:

(a) Select a short story and write a paragraph character sketch of a person in the story

(b) Given a list of short stories, select two for analysis and then

(1) Name two characters from the stories who were forced to make a decision (cite title and page)

(2) For the two in (1) above give a written analysis of how that decision was made and how the decision influenced the life of the person

(3) Name one character who experienced success (title and page) and explain in writing how success influenced the life of that person, citing events in the story to substantiate your position

(4) Name one character who experienced failure (title and page) and explain in writing how failure influenced the life of that person, citing events in the story to substantiate your position.

Indicate, by placing a **C** for closed or an **O** for open, the type of each behavior listed in the Terminal Behavioral Objective above.

(a)_____

(b)(1)_____

" (2)_____

" (3)_____

" (4)_____

I marked all of them **O** as each learner's response could show originality or be different from other learner's responses.

If the learner is expected to:
1. name the parts of a flower
2. add 36, 29 and 42
3. label a drawing
4. underline the nouns once and subject twice
5. circle the modifiers in a sentence
6. list the first ten articles of the Constitution
7. choose the best definition from three given for a certain term
8. mark T or F after judging a statement
9. and express other similar behaviors,

then, if these behaviors were expressed as objectives, would the objectives be *open* or *closed?* (choose one)

If there was no question in your mind that all the above behaviors called for exactly the same responses from all learners then you have perceived the idea of *closed* behaviors.

If the learner is expected to:
1. summarize a story of his choice
2. develop a design for a model airplane
3. originate two hypotheses and gather evidence to support them
4. write sentences using a certain type of modifier
5. plan a week's menu for a family of four
6. draw up a model law or set of laws for drug control
7. outline a book report
8. develop a series of tests of physical fitness
9. and express other similar behaviors,

then, if these behaviors were expressed as objectives, would the objectives be *open* or *closed?* (choose one)

_____

Again, if there was no question in your mind that all the above
behaviors called for original or variable learner responses then you
have perceived the idea of *open* behaviors.

_____

The one thing remaining for you to do as part of this section is to
develop some objectives for yourself that are open, closed or part open
and part closed. Complete the following three objectives by write-in
of a behavior for each.

1. (Make this one *closed*)
   Learner is to differentiate between subjects and predicates so that
   when given twenty sentences he can

   _____

   _____

   _____

2. (Make this one *open*)
   Learner is to differentiate between subjects and predicates so that
   he can

   _____

   _____

   _____

3. (Make this one *open* and *closed*)
   Learner is to differentiate between subjects and predicates so that
   he can:

   a. _____

   _____

   _____

   b. _____

   _____

   _____

Here is the way I completed these three objectives.

1. (closed) Learner is to differentiate between subjects and predicates so that when given twenty sentences he can *underline the subject of each once and the predicate twice.*

2. (open) Learner is to differentiate between subjects and predicates so that he can *using a newspaper of his choice locate ten sentences and tell for each which word or words are the subject and which word or words are the predicate.*

3. (open and closed) Learner is to differentiate between subjects and predicates so that he can:
   (a) *when given ten sentences with blanks for subject and predicate, properly fill in the blanks to make complete sentences*
   (b) *create ten complete sentences.*

The criterion test for this section is next. You will be expected to analyze three objectives marking the behaviors as open or closed and then to create three objectives of your own.

Criterion Test—Section 8

Part I.

In each of the three objectives below there are two or more behaviors. Following the objectives (below) you will find space to record your answers. Classify each behavior a, b, c, etc., as open or closed.

TBO 1. Learner is to develop an understanding of the concept of open and closed objectives so that he can:
   a. when given three objectives analyze each behavior, and classify it, by marking **O** or **C**, as an open or a closed objective, and
   b. create one example each of open, closed and open and closed objectives.

TBO 2. Learner is to develop skill in listening so that he can:
   a. copy five orally dictated words correctly
   b. when exposed to twelve sounds classify them as loud or soft, and as vocal or non-vocal
   c. keep time to a variety of rhythms when listening to a tape recording of changing rhythmic music.

TBO 3. Learner is to develop an understanding of the structure, organization and content of unabridged dictionaries and skill in using them so that he can:
   a. when given five words, divide them correctly into syllables

b. when given five sentences with an underlined term, write the meaning of the words as used in context
c. when given five words, write as many synonyms as he can for the terms
d. when given two words, write a variant spelling of the terms
e. when given five words, list the parts of speech each can be used as
f. when given five prefixes, write the meaning of the prefixes
g. when given five words, classify them as modern, obsolete, or archaic
h. locate five words new to him and create a sentence for each, using the term correctly.

_____

Record Your Answers Here:

3. a. _____

1. a. _____
                        b. _____

   b. _____
                        c. _____

                        d. _____

2. a. _____
                        e. _____

   b. _____
                        f. _____

   c. _____
                        g. _____

                        h. _____

Part II.

In the spaces below write three original objectives illustrating open, closed, and open and closed.

1. (closed)

2. (open)

3. (open and closed)

Answers to Criterion Test — Section 8 in Appendix A-7, p. 100.

9

How Do I Know
My Objective Is Good?

TERMINAL BEHAVIORAL OBJECTIVE: *Learner is to understand the concept of goodness or validity as it relates to an objective so that he can: (a) list the four major purposes of an objective; (b) write an objective and analyze it for "goodness" in relation to the four purposes, listing the points of the analysis in writing.*

Goodness is very difficult to "pin down" as there are a variety of ways in which an objective could be considered good, as:

1. Good for the learner, meaning useful
2. Good for the learner, meaning enjoyable
3. Good for the learner, necessary later
4. Good for the learner, high vocational utility
5. Good for the learner, in the sense that it is "easy"
6. Good for the learner, meaning he achieved it or was successful with it
7. Good in the sense it has cultural application
8. Good in the eyes of experts
9. Good in the judgment of the average person—it sounds reasonable
10. Good in the sense that it is frequently called for—frequency of use

Implicit in the above ten ways that an objective might be good are the ways to test the *goodness* of an objective.

Goodness in a more technical sense is related to the concept of validity. Validity is always relative—relative to some predefined purpose. In this sense an objective is good (valid) if it does well what it was intended it should do. Therefore, to determine if an objective is good we must ask, "How well is it accomplishing its purpose?"

Objectives are developed to: (1) communicate ideas to others, (2) serve as a base for selecting instructional activities, (3) serve as a base for evaluating learning, (4) define useful behaviors to be accomplished by learners. Objectives should meet all four of these purposes if they are to be good.

Let's examine each of the four purposes separately.

If an objective communicates it is generally read (used) by teachers and/or learners. Written expressions of objectives communicate if the teacher or the learner, after reading the objective, knows exactly what the author intended and can interpret the objective in the same way as other readers. A simple test of communication goodness is to have two or more readers interpret it. If different interpretations occur, then it is failing to communicate properly.

As an example, let us consider this objective:

Learners are to develop an understanding of 200 technical vocabulary terms and be able to use them.

We ask teacher X what this objective means and she tells us the student is to *use* each term by *constructing a sentence* for each one (220 sentences in all). We ask teacher Y what this objective means and she tells us that in *any type of oral or written expression* (essay) the learners are to *use* appropriate technical terminology. In this case it is obvious that the objective, as originally written, failed to communicate, as teachers X and Y each interpreted the term "use" to mean something different.

This same problem could happen to learners, in which case they would develop a behavior according to their interpretation of the objective when the teacher expects a behavior in a different form. It is likely that the learner would be penalized for having the wrong behavior through no fault of his own.

The second purpose of an objective is to serve as a base for selecting appropriate learning activities.

If an objective is not clear, then the way to implement the objective must remain unclear. Using an illustration of a vague objective we have this problem:

Learners are to know 200 technical vocabulary terms.

As you already have learned, this objective has no primary or secondary behavior. *To know* does not state what the learner is to *do* at the end of the instructional period. In this case how can the teacher be sure that she has devised the proper learning setting? What are the learners doing in the classroom to prepare themselves for the kind of behavior expected of them at the end? Teacher X may decide to drill the students on spelling, pronouncing and memorizing dictionary definitions of the terms while teacher Y has her learners working on defining the terms in the learner's own words and applying the terms correctly in class discussions. Here we see a wide variation in the *learning activities* leading to what the teachers believe to be their own particular interpretation of the behaviors appropriate to "knowing."

In an efficient learning situation it should be apparent that a good behavioral objective will aid the teacher in selecting the *proper* learning activities. It is obvious that if learners are expected to use technical terms in sentences the learning activities will be different than if the learners are to recite standard definitions. The objective should state a specific behavior as "—use technical terms in sentences," or "—recite standard definitions."

To summarize this second point, we can only say, "how do you get there (terminal behaviors) if you don't know where you are going?"

The third purpose of an objective is to serve as a base for evaluating learning as shown in the simple diagram above. Implicit in the behavioral objective is the evaluation of its accomplishment. That is, the overt behavior called for in the objective is the behavior to be demonstrated by the learner at the end of the learning period. This is why *end* objectives are called *terminal behavioral objectives*.

Notice that the test or evaluation is not directly specified in the objective. For example, this would be a poor objective:

> Learner is to know fifty nouns and how to use them so that he can pass a written test of fifty items with forty-five correct answers.

The reason this objective is poor is because the only behavior required is to *pass a test*. This is not a behavior generally required in life nor the end product of learning. We don't run around after leaving school "passing tests." Also, "pass a test" is vague. What exactly does it mean? Is it checking, writing, underlining, choosing, or some other test behavior? *To know* is not a behavior—*passing a test* is at best a very vague, loose description of a behavior; both are covert—no specific, overt behavior is required in the above example. Here is another example, equally poor:

> Learner is to understand how to use fifty nouns so that he can choose (mark with an X) the correct sentence, in forty-five out of fifty multiple choice test items, which demonstrate the correct use of the noun.

The objective is poorly designed because the secondary behavior (mark with an X) is to stand for the primary behavior *use*. Marking with an X is not valid; it does not prove the learner can use. In addition, *use* is a vague term. How do we get around this problem? In the first place, do not specify a test behavior; in the second, be sure the secondary behavior is valid; and in the third, be sure the primary behavior is specific. For example, the objective could be written as:

> The learner is to understand how to use fifty nouns correctly in writing by being able to construct (write) twenty sentences using at least twenty of the fifty nouns correctly.

The primary behavior is *use correctly in writing* and the secondary behavior is to *construct (write)*. The secondary behavior is valid and appropriate. No test is described but it is very implicit. The evaluation will require the learner to construct (write) a minimum of twenty sentences. Several different tests could be devised to meet this required behavior.

It should be apparent by now that a good objective is a base for evaluating because the evaluation required is *clearly implicit* in the objective.

So far in section 9 we have discussed three of the four major purposes of an objective and how the concept of goodness or validity is related to each.

Remember, a good objective is determined by how well it carries out or meets its *intended purpose*.

We have covered the purposes of:
1. communication
2. base for selecting instructional activities
3. base for selecting evaluation activity

Stop here and *think* about goodness as related to these 3 purposes. How is goodness achieved for each purpose?

The fourth and final purpose of an objective is to *define useful behaviors to be accomplished by learners.* This is a rather broad purpose and individuals will not agree as to whether a given objective is useful or not.

What is meant by the term *useful?* The easiest way to think about it is to view usefulness as either *technological* or *philosophical* usefulness. Another way to say the same thing is to ask: Does the objective have a *technological* application or *philosophical* value? If you answer "no" to both, then the objective probably is not good. If either a technological application or a philosophical value is achieved by the behavior specified in the objective, then it can be considered good.

Technological application means that the objective calls for a behavior which will serve the learner as: (a) a basic skill, (b) a vocational skill, or (c) a useful behavior in some aspect of living as relating to his survival in our culture (marriage, filling out income tax forms, purchasing groceries, etc.).

Philosophical value means that the objective calls for a behavior which will be useful to the learner as it enhances his: (a) enjoyment, (b) interests, (c) values, (d) appreciations.

Let's go through a simple validity analysis of two objectives and see if the four purposes of an objective can be met by the examples as designed.

Example 1.   (Assume this to be an objective in a college level,
                       advanced, elective course.)

Learner is to select and analyze critically one work each of Elizabethan and Romantic poetry, both choices excluding examples used in class, and to write a summary of his analysis.

Analyzing this objective for validity of the four purposes: Communication, base for evaluation, base of instructional activity selection, and presence of useful behaviors.

Q1: Does the objective communicate clearly?
Answer: Yes and no. The primary behavior *analyze* is not entirely clear unless the basis of the analysis is made known. The secondary behavior, *write a summary*, is probably clear enough as it would not be necessary to have the summary in a definite format.

Q2: Does the objective imply the instructional activity needed?
Answer: Yes. In-class and extra-class learning would center around analyzing examples of Elizabethan and Romantic poetry using some criteria for analysis. Learners would either learn the criteria first or learn as they proceed to analyze.

Q3: Does the objective imply the evaluation needed?
Answer: Yes. Learner would be required to select two examples and write a summary of his analysis.

Q4: Does the objective serve a useful purpose?
Answer: Yes. Everyone wouldn't need this behavior but this is at college level, an advanced course, and the course is elective, not required (those in the course should find either a technological or philosophical use for the behavior).

Summary: Objective needs redesigning. The new design should indicate in some way the points to be included in an analysis—the criteria for the analysis.

Now let's try again with another objective.
Example 2. (college level, advanced, required course in teacher-training)

Learners are to understand and apply eleven basic components of teaching as listed in the Manual, A-1 by demonstrating each component through a 4-5-minute micro-teach sequence as outlined in the manual.

Q1: Does the objective communicate clearly?
Answer: Yes. The eleven things to be understood and applied are listed as well as all other necessary information.

Q2: Does the objective imply the instructional activities needed?
Answer: Yes. It is logically clear the learner will: first, know the components; second, study them thoroughly; third, learn how to go through a micro-teach; fourth, practice a micro-teach; and finally, apply a micro-teach to each component.

Q3: Does the objective imply the evaluation needed?
Answer: Yes. He is to teach each component and the how-to-do-it is listed as well as the time.

Q4:   Does the objective serve a useful purpose?
Answer: Yes. It is developing teaching skills in teachers (a vocational skill).

Practice your skill!

Self Check Test

List four general purposes served by an objective.

1.

2.

3.

4.

Now, for the next objective analyze, by written comment, its goodness relative to the four purposes:

Terminal Behavioral Objective (required, high school biology):

> Learners are to develop skill in setting up, focusing, and viewing through a microscope so that when given a prepared slide of a simple micro object they can sketch an outline of the object.

Q1: Does the objective communicate clearly?
Answer:

Q2: Does the objective imply the instructional activity needed?
Answer:

Q3: Does the objective imply the evaluation needed?
Answer:

Q4: Does the objective serve a useful purpose?
Answer:

Answers to the Self Check Test:

The four general purposes served by an objective are: (1) communication, (2) as a base for evaluation, (3) as a base for selecting instructional activities, (4) usefulness.

Your written analysis: There is no exact answer but this objective would probably get a *yes* to all four purposes.

Criterion Test—Section 9

Part I.   List the four major purposes served by an objective.

   1.

   2.

   3.

   4.

       ą Terminal Behavioral Objective and tell the grade/
       ɹd course for which it is intended.

Terminal Behavioral Objective:

(course and level:

Part III. Analyze in writing the objective you just designed as to its goodness in relation to the four purposes.

Q1:
Answer:

Q2:
Answer:

Q3:
Answer:

Q4:
Answer:

(Note: There is no standard answer with which to compare yours.)

10

How Do I Use
My Objective?

TERMINAL BEHAVIORAL OBJECTIVE: *Learners are to under-*
stand the purpose or func-
tions of objectives so that
they can briefly explain
each in a short, written
paragraph.

In section 9 you learned how to use your judgment in determining the value or goodness of an objective. In prior sections you learned
from a mechanical point-of-view how to design and express objectives
in writing. Now that you can generate objectives it is appropriate to
gain insight into the role they can play—and it is a rather powerful one
—in improving learning.

Very briefly, let's return to a point made early in this manual:

LEARNING IS CHANGE IN BEHAVIOR.

Now we have made quite an issue about *who it is that is to do the learning—the students!* If students are to learn effectively it is only logical
that they: (a) Know what it is they are to learn, (b) Perceive how
they are to learn and (c) Have some concept of when their learning
is complete.

It is readily apparent that objectives will help the student with
all three of the above:

    a. Objectives can be used to inform learners as to *what they are*
       to learn.

    b. Objectives, as you learned in section 9, will aid in selecting the
       proper instructional activities, so the learner benefits in *know-*
       ing how he is to learn.

c. Objectives, as you also learned in section 9, clearly imply the way the learning is to be evaluated, so the learner benefits by knowing exactly what is to be expected by way of a *test* or *proof* that he has learned.

It was also pointed out, in section 9, that one purpose of an objective is to communicate. Objectives then—especially Terminal Behavioral Objectives—can be used to:

Communicate to Learners—(a) what they are to learn, and (b) exactly what behaviors they should have when their learning is complete.

It should not be necessary to furnish learners with a list of objectives expressed exactly as you would for professional purposes. That is, the formal expressions of objectives may not be what they need. Instead a rewritten version may be presented to them. Here is an example of what we mean:

Terminal Behavioral Objective:
Learners are to understand how to use nouns correctly in writing (have the correct meaning in context) so that they can write twenty sentences using twenty nouns correctly of the fifty nouns listed.

For the learner, his assignment sheet might read as follows:
At the end of this lesson you are to know the meaning of the fifty nouns listed below. You will be expected to write a minimum of twenty sentences using twenty of the fifty nouns correctly. The twenty nouns will be selected by the teacher.

Communicating to Professional Educators—a second use for objectives.

Continuing with the subject of an objective *communicating*, objectives are also used to communicate to other professional people. Communication through objectives is valuable in preparing manuals, text books, courses of study and curriculum guides, as well as in program planning, research and in designing all types of teaching aids and materials.

Using even a small illustration—an "educational toy," say—we ask the question: For what purpose was it developed? If I used this toy in teaching, what change could I expect in the learner? That is, what objectives could the toy help the learner achieve? What is the purpose of the toy? So, the objectives of courses, materials and aids should be enumerated if the user is expected to get the most from them.

Further, a curriculum guide is relatively useless unless the teacher can determine exactly what behaviors the curriculum is expected to develop.

A third function of objectives is to aid the teacher or curriculum developer in selecting appropriate learning activities. [This point was mentioned in section 9.] Perhaps you recall the diagram which indicated:

This diagram illustrates that once the end point of instruction is specific it makes possible the intelligent selection of learning activities. Good teachers are constantly seeking ways to improve their instruction which means they are looking for ways and means to: (a) reduce instructional time, (b) improve end of learning performance, (c) improve delayed retention, (d) improve *pre-learning* and *during learning* motivation.

At present, many learners are required to participate in learning activities unrelated to any specific goals. These activities need to be eliminated. They are commonly referred to as "busy work." Additionally, some learning activities are more appropriate than others and should be employed if it is at all possible to do so. Specifying the learning behaviors enhances the probability that appropriate learning activities will be selected. To illustrate the point, assume the following objective has been developed for 7th grade Life Science:

Terminal Behavioral Objective:
> The learners are to develop skill in the written, contextual use of 90 percent of the technical terms as listed in the *Glossary* of the text so that they can when given any set of twenty terms, construct a sentence which uses each term properly.

This terminal behavioral objective suggests that the instruction must somehow provide:

a. opportunity to learn how to spell the terms
b. practice in spelling the terms
c. self checking on their ability to spell the terms
d. opportunity to learn the meaning of the terms
e. opportunity to "personalize" the meaning of the terms
f. opportunity to use (write) the terms in context

g. self-checking on their ability to use the terms correctly in written context.

If an objective is improperly designed the instructional activities may be randomly selected and then only by chance may the activities be relevant. Here is an illustration:

Improperly Designed Terminal Behavioral Objective:
Learners are to develop an understanding of the technical terms as listed in the *Glossary* of the text.

Teacher X may decide the instruction should:
a. provide drill in spelling
b. provide opportunity for student to memorize dictionary definition of the term.

Teacher Y may decide the instruction should:
a. provide practice in using the terms correctly in oral conversation.

Teacher Z may decide the instruction should:
a. provide opportunity for learner to derive the meaning of the terms through root and contextual analysis
b. provide opportunity for students to create their own definitions of the terms.

Now, all three teachers may assign some written work and then "mark off" the student's grade whenever the student has used a term improperly in writing. However, not one of the three teachers in our example provided the opportunity for their learners to acquire the writing behavior during the instructional period. In this case, the students didn't "luck out!"

We have now established three functions of objectives: (1) Communicate to learners, (2) Communicate to other members of the teaching profession, (3) Aid teachers in selecting proper instructional activities.

A fourth function of objectives is they can serve as a base for selecting appropriate evaluations of learning. Implicit in good objectives is the test (proof of acquisition of the behavior) of the learner's having achieved that which is specified. In a well designed objective the overt behavioral description implies the evaluation as in this example:

Terminal Behavioral Objective:
Learners are to understand the functions of objectives so that they can *name* five functions and briefly explain each in a short, *written* paragraph.

How could anyone (teacher) fail to know how to evaluate this objective? The learner obviously is going to be required at the end of learning to:

a. name five functions served by objectives

b. write a short paragraph explaining each function.

We say the evaluation is *implicit* or *implied* because the test (evaluation) is not formally described as such. For example, this is *wrong:*

> Learners are to understand the functions of objectives so that they can pass a test asking them to name and explain each function.

Why is it wrong? The phrase "pass a test" also is a behavior, even if vague, and therefore the objective appears to emphasize the development of a "test-passing behavior" which is not the intent of the objective.

When the primary behavior is overt and well expressed, the evaluation is implied as:

> Learners are to develop skill in typing so that they can average 50 w/m for 5 minutes from copy.

The primary behavior is *type* so the learner will be required to *type*.

When the primary behavior is covert a secondary, overt behavior implies the evaluation as:

> Learners are to develop skill in *adding* so that they can *record* the sums of 10, two column addition problems.

The primary behavior is *add,* which cannot be observed. The secondary behavior is *record* which can be observed, or the results of the recording observed. In this case the evaluation is obvious, in that the learner will be given ten two-column addition problems with space to record his answers.

In the affective domain your objectives may specify limited, imperfect, or even no behaviors. In this case, the evaluation is correspondingly limited, imperfect or even lacking. When evaluations are demanded, as by administrative policy, then the evaluator generally resorts to subjective evaluation techniques.

A fifth function of objectives is that they are public records of what is to be learned and therefore open to the question of "how useful are they?" In section 9, we discussed *usefulness* in terms of being *technologically* useful or *philosophically* useful. What is being taught (learned) in school cannot be judged if any of the following conditions exist:

    a. teachers don't know what the learners are to do

    b. pupils don't know what they are to do

    c. there is no formal attempt to describe what is to be learned (no list of objectives)

    d. objectives are vague or general and not clear and specific.

This function should be clear without further elaboration.

Can you name the five functions of an objective? Try to recall them. If you can't, review the appropriate parts of this section.

Can you tell how each function of an objective is related to the objective? Try to describe the relationship in your own words. If you can't, review the appropriate parts of this section.

Criterion Test—Section 10

Part I.   Name five functions or purposes of an objective and describe each function in a short paragraph.

1.

2.

3.

4.

5.

Answers to Criterion Test — Section 10 in Appendix A-8, pp. 100-101.

11

What Are Experience Objectives?

TERMINAL BEHAVIORAL OBJECTIVE: *Learner is to understand the concept of experience objectives so that he can, in his own words, define and briefly describe what they are.*

No volume would be complete without a section explaining the exception to the rule. This section deals with such an exception. Up to this point we have structured, analyzed, evaluated and classified objectives as if all learning in life was amenable to this process. Most learning is! However, many educators claim that there are some things they want their learners to acquire that just do not fit any set of standards or system of classification. I agree with them. Sometimes in teaching you want the learners to go through *some experience* just for the sake of the experience itself. You may be personally convinced that the learner will learn something (change his behavior as a result of the experience) but you are not concerned with the what, the how or the why of the change(s). You could not, nor do you want to specify any specific behaviors which are to be the result of the learner's experience.

To accomodate this type of objective (if it is a type) we need to recognize another category in addition to the nine classes (K, U, P, S, At, Ap, In, M, MO) as defined and explained in section 5 of this volume. This type of objective we are calling an EXPERIENCE OBJECTIVE.

An *experience objective* is a required situation, structured or nonstructured, participated in by a learner. The outcome of the objective is whatever has been uniquely perceived, assimilated and internalized by the learner as a result of the experience.

How are such objectives worded? Do experience objectives have to meet the requirements of terminal behavioral objectives?

An experience objective is not verbally expressed as a terminal behavioral objective as the teacher is not interested in specifying a behavioral outcome. Instead, an experience objective is described; the experience in which the learner is to participate is described in whatever way the instructor desires. Some experience objectives are structured and some are more or less unstructured.

Let's look at two examples so that the meaning of what an experience objective is, is clearer.

Example 1:

Learner is to live, upon assignment, with a Mexican-American family in the barrios for a two week period.

The experience of living with a Mexican-American family is an experience we have decided we want our prospective teachers to have. The objective facilitates the preparation of teachers, in our estimation, because the trainees who have been through this experience almost unanimously report it as worthwhile. What did they get out of it? Well, different trainees have reported different results as:

Prospective Teacher X — "I have a much greater respect for Mexican-American mothers."

Prospective Teacher Y — "I never realized how little (money) some families have to live on. I don't see how they do it."

Prospective Teacher Z — "I just loved those kids!"

Suppose some teacher trainee, after this "experience" decided he (or she) were "in the wrong program" and "wanted out." This would still be a valuable outcome (to the trainee) but certainly not something the instructor would anticipate and want to describe or specify as a terminal behavior.

Example 2:

Learner is to participate in at least three of the informal group discussions concerning teacher-administrator relationships.

If a teacher trainer were to write this experience objective as a terminal behavioral objective and add something like "so that he can write a description of the ideal relationship which should exist between teacher-principal, . . .," this might *kill* the things (whatever they are) that could be learned or gained from the discussion. Humans are leary about putting their feelings down on paper for public viewing and knowing they are going to be required to do so could *prevent* or *color* their ability to *feel* about the topic discussed and destroy the whole intent of the discussion.

Hopefully at this point you understand what an experience objective is:

A required, structured or nonstructured situation, participated in by a learner, for which no specific terminal behaviors have been specified.

The general idea of experience objectives is not hard to convey or to understand. The exact nature of such objectives is difficult to explain since they vary widely. Here are some additional examples that have been required of learners.

Some Typical Experience Objectives:

1. You are required to attend the Friday Brown Bag Lunches for the month of April.
2. Learner will attend the V.D. seminar on February____, 197__, scheduled in Suite A of the S.U.B. at 2:00 P.M.
3. During the period of your practice teaching you will be expected to attend all faculty meetings of the school to which you are assigned.
4. For the period of your training you will be expected to meet regularly with your advisor for informal counseling.
5. During the summer, prior to your internship, you will be required to spend a minimum of three weeks to a maximum of three months working with youngsters at Camp_____. The actual length of time and period of work should be arranged with Dr._____ during the week of April 13-17 in Room 610.

Criterion Test—Section 11

1. Define or tell in your own words what an experience objective is.

2. Briefly describe an experience objective and tell its purpose.

Answers to Criterion Test Section 11 in Appendix A-9, p. 101.

12

Show Me
Some Examples

It helps to have some leads, clues, or examples to go by when developing objectives. After all, it is a creative writing process and most of us need examples to shake ideas loose in our minds. It is not the intent of this volume to be a source book of objectives, so only a limited number of examples of objectives which fulfill the criteria described in this volume can be provided. Each of the examples is a *Terminal Behavioral Objective* (TBO) and will be labeled as to level and field. Hopefully, at the end of this section you will be on your own and will develop a set (list) of objectives for some course, subject, or area of instruction.

Primary — Reading

TBO–1. Learner is to understand the likenesses and differences between printed symbols so that he can:
   a. Match individual letters or simple words on the basis of their shape
   b. Match upper and lower case letters of the alphabet
   c. Match pictures with spoken words
   d. Match objects or abstract symbols which are alike in mixed groups of objects or symbols
   e. Speak a word and match it with a printed object.

Primary — Grammar

TBO–2. Learner is to know nouns and pronouns so that he can identify them in lists or sentences by:
   a. Checking the nouns (or pronouns) in a given list of words
   b. Checking the nouns (or pronouns) in simple sentences
   c. Checking the common nouns in a list of words and in a list of words restricted to common and proper nouns
   d. Checking the personal pronouns in a list of words and in a list of words restricted to personal and indefinite pronouns

e. Checking the personal and indefinite pronouns in simple sentences.

Primary — Science

TBO—3. Learner is to develop an understanding of and skill in using a classification system for real objects so that he can devise a system of his own utilizing the factors (elements) of living (organic), non-living (inorganic), odor, texture, size, shape, weight, temperature, color, and taste to group 75 to 100 individual objects into subsets.

Primary — Science

TBO—4. Learner is to know selected concepts pertaining to water; that it is a liquid, it freezes to a solid, is used by living things, it acts as a solvent, and it evaporates; so that he can, for each concept, devise a way to observe related phenomena, make the observation, and communicate his observations orally to peer group.

Primary — Mathematics

TBO—5. Learner is to understand how to construct and read graphs so that he can:
a. Complete a list of data, with blanks, by reading a simple bar graph and a picture graph
b. Construct a simple bar graph and a picture graph to depict a given set of data
c. Locate the typical set of data (median) in a bell-shaped distribution as depicted in a bar graph, picture graph, and a polygon.

Primary — Science/Math

TBO—6. Learner is to understand the concept of measurement so that he can:
a. Orally name five measuring instruments
b. Name one or more units or fractions of units for each instrument named in a (above)
c. When given three objects or problems complete a linear measurement of each in inches and feet
d. When given a container of water, record its temperature
e. Record the elapsed time in seconds of an interval between two successive sounds.

Primary — History

TBO—7. Learner is to understand the concept of community growth and development so that he can:
a. Propose two ways (factors) to measure growth of a given community
b. Gather and present in writing data in support of a (above)

    c. List five changes that have taken place in the last ten years in his own community (information may be personally observed or gained by communicating with others)

    d. Judge the changes listed in c (above) as being either advantageous or disadvantageous to him and be able to explain orally the reasons why.

Primary — Economics

TBO—8. Learner is to understand concepts relating to the need and provisions for human shelter so that he can:

    a. Orally name and explain a minimum of four reasons why humans need shelter

    b. Orally name assorted pictures of shelter types from around the world

    c. Orally name a minimum of ten materials used for building shelters (rock, logs, cement, cloth, glass, furs or skin, sod, steel, brick, boards, tile, etc.).

Middle School — Grammar

TBO—12. Learner is to develop an understanding of concepts relating to, and skill in the use of sentence structure and sentence writing so that he can:

    a. Given a list of sentences classify them as declarative, imperative, interrogative, or exclamatory

    b. Select a story and find two examples of each sentence type as in a (above)

    c. Construct two examples of each sentence type as in a (above)

    d. Given three pairs of sentences, rewrite each pair as one sentence

    e. Given five declarative sentences, underline the whole subject and whole predicate

    f. Construct two sentences of examples of each of the following sentence patterns: N-V, N-V-N, N-LV-N, and N-LV-AD.

Middle School — Physics

TBO—13. Learner is to develop an understanding of the relationship between molecules and heat as a form of energy so that he can:

    a. Describe evaporation in molecular terms and logically explain why it is a cooling process

    b. Describe changes in state in molecular terms

    c. Devise and conduct a demonstration writing up the results relative to:

      1) Water, heat and effect on solubility of common salts

      2) Metals, heat and effect on volume

    d. Read a variety of chemical, household and clinical thermometers and record temperatures in both F° and C° scales.

Middle School — Biology

TBO—14. Learner is to understand concepts relative to plant reproduction so that he can:
  a. Label the stamen, anther, pistil, stigma, ovary, style, pollen, pollen tube, sepals and petals in a diagram of a typical flower
  b. Define in writing: layering, budding, spore formation, fission, fusion and vegative in relation to reproduction
  c. Describe in writing self- and cross-pollination
  d. List the characteristics of sexual and asexual reproduction.

Middle School — General Mathematics

TBO—15. Learner is to understand concepts relating to linear and square dimensional relationships and skill in solving type problems relating to regular and irregular geometric figures as triangle, squares, rectangles, circles and five-, six- and eight-dimensional polygons so that he can:
  a. When given the dimensions of any polygon and the area formula, find the area of the figure
  b. When given the area and any one dimension and the area formula of any polygon find the other dimension
  c. Find the perimeter of any regular or irregular polygon when given the dimensions or by measuring actual figures
  d. Find the circumference and area of a circle when given the formula and the radius.

Middle School — General Mathematics

TBO—16. Learner is to understand the concept of central tendency so that he can:
  a. Given a set of data, compute the mean
  b. Given a set of data, locate the mode
  c. Given a set of data, compute the median
  d. Show by drawing a diagram the relationship between M, Mdn, and M_0 in symmetrical bell-shaped, symmetrical U-shaped and skewed bell-shaped distributions
  e. Demonstrate, by solving an original example, the effect of including either one unusually high and one unusually low score in a common set of data on the three measures of central tendency
  f. Describe, in simulated problems, the effect of stating the median only or the mean only when referring to "average."

Middle School — Research Analysis Skill

TBO—17. Learner is to develop skill in analyzing written or recorded statements so that he can:
  a. Given five sentences or paragraph pairs, judge whether the statements are fact or opinion

b. Locate in newspapers or magazines five examples each of statements of fact and statements of opinion
c. Locate a written example of objective and nonobjective style of writing
d. Listen to four recorded short essays and classify them as objective or nonobjective
e. Locate three concluding statements in written essays
f. Locate three premise statements in written essays
g. Locate three examples of statements of hidden meaning in advertising
h. Develop an original list of thirty terms which could be used regularly to influence emotional set in the reader
i. Devise a check list or rating scale to evaluate written material on an emotion-objective continuum.

Middle School — History

TBO—18. Learner is to understand the past and present causes and trends related to urban growth in the United States so that he can:
a. Devise a rural-urban population graph by decade (1920-70) using official census data
b. Trace the total population growth (decline) and the rural-urban shift for four states (one each in West, Midwest, East and South) of your choice and graph the data. Write a summary report of your findings including conclusions and trends
c. Locate information and write a summary report about current or proposed urban improvement plans and programs
d. Using United States Census data and a current population density map redraw the map predicting the 1980 and 2000 population density picture
e. List and explain the current migration patterns in the United States including urban-rural, inner city-suburb, black-white, interregional and international shifts
f. Select an ethnic group and trace its population patterns in the United States and explain how these are related to social problems
g. Select one factor in urban location and development (water, transportation route, natural resource supply, etc.) and then judge how this factor influenced the location of our twenty-five largest cities
h. Select one city you believe to depend to a significant degree on tourism for its income, locate as much information about this city as you can and show how its peculiar location and subsequent growth is related to recreation and service
i. Trace the effect of the Civil War, World War I and World War II on birth rate by graphing the rates for the years 1860-75 inclusive, 1915-30 inclusive and 1940-65 inclusive.

Middle School — Economics

TBO—19. Learner is to understand the relationship between energy production and industrial growth so that he can:
   a. Graph the fossil fuel (coal) production in the United States 1910-70 inclusive
   b. Graph the electrical output in the United States 1910-70 inclusive
   c. Graph the oil production and consumption in the United States 1910-70 inclusive
   d. Graph the natural gas production in the United States 1910-70 inclusive
   e. Graph the GNP for the United States 1910-70 inclusive
   f. Graph the current reserves for oil, natural gas and coal
   g. Write a short explanation of the relationship between energy produced and industrial production from 1910 to date
   h. Graph the steel production, auto production and rail car loadings per year for years 1920-70 inclusive
   i. Locate sources and write a summary of the current and future energy needs of the United States.

Middle School — Political Science

TBO—20. Learner is to understand the relationship between federal, state and local government and the tax structure so that he can:
   a. Graph both the total and percent increase in federal, state (yours) and local tax income for the decades 1900-70 inclusive
   b. Graph the total number and percent of employees in federal, state (yours) and local government for the decades 1900-70 inclusive
   c. Develop pie graphs of the total local government expenditures and the source of income (local, state and federal) for the decades 1930-70
   d. Write a summary paper including conclusions with supporting data, relative to federal, state (yours), and local rates of growth, income from taxes and future trends in these areas.

Secondary — Research Skills

TBO—21. Learner is to locate, evaluate, synthesize and construct a research paper so that he can:
   a. Select a topic of his choice that is limited in scope, yet researchable
   b. Locate a minimum of five sources from a library card catalog pertaining to his topic and list them in acceptable bibliographic form
   c. Locate a minimum of five sources using the *Reader's Guide to Periodical Literature* and prepare bibliography cards

d. Organize and write a research paper meeting the requirements of all the elements listed in the handbook *Form and Style*.

Secondary — Creative Writing

TBO—22. Learner is to develop skill in creative writing so that he can;
  a. Select a controversial topic of interest to teenagers
  b. Using the topic in a (above), create a minimum of 200-300 word dialogue between two young people of the same sex about the topic
  c. Repeat b (above) with the dialogue between two young people of the opposite sex
  d. Select any three events within these categories
    1) adjustment
    2) conflict
    3) danger
    4) failure
    5) jinx
    6) luck
    7) resistance
    8) success
    9) sorrow
    10) tragedy
    that you have personally observed and write two descriptive paragraphs which pertain to each event
  e. Write a character sketch of someone younger than you and someone older than you
  f. Write an objective report concerning some observed incident—an automobile accident, a happening at a sporting event, etc. (length not important).

Secondary — Physical Science

TBO—23. Learner is to understand the concept of continental drift so that he can:
  a. Using current cutout outlines of the continents, place them into a single mass
  b. Describe how current physical phenomena are the result of drift and collision
  c. Trace the drift of land masses from their beginning and predict where they will be 1 million years from now
  d. Write a brief explanation of how the Rocky Mountain, Himalayan, and Pyrenean ranges have risen as a result of continental drift.

Secondary — Physical Science

TBO—24. Learner is to understand concepts and relationships between weather and climate, present and past, so that he can:
  a. Diagram the water cycle and write an explanation of how it operates

b. Write an explanation of how air masses form and move, and their effect on current weather

c. Cite known evidence relating to long range cycles of weather and cycles of climate

d. Write a description of the changes which would be produced on the globe with a long range increase in average temperature

e. Predict what effect there would be on the earth with a significant increase in cloud cover, smog and carbon dioxide content of the atmosphere

f. Predict what effect there would be on the earth with a significant decrease in the ozone layer and a decrease in cloud cover

g. Investigate and write a report on high altitude winds, the cause of their formation and their effects on the earth's weather and climate.

Secondary — Geometry

TBO–25. Learner is to develop skill in depicting geometric figures so that when given a compass, straightedge marker and a protractor he can construct right, acute, obtuse, straight, supplementary and complementary angles; draw lines perpendicular, construct perpendiculars from points to lines; divide angles and lines into segments; construct all types of triangles; construct regular and irregular polygons; construct parallelograms; construct circles, tangents and axes; construct one angle which equals the sum of two given angles; construct rectangles which are the equivalent of the sums of the areas of two given rectangles; and from word problems which involve measuring and construction, solve the problems.

Secondary — Statistics

TBO–26. Learner is to understand concepts relating to the normal curve and solve problems involving area relationships under the curves so that when given a three place table of $\frac{X}{\sigma}$ values he can:

a. Find the area between the mean ordinate and an ordinate erected at a given σ distance from the mean

b. Given the general problem with $\underline{M}=\underline{X}$, $\sigma=\underline{Y}$, N=$\underline{Z}$, determine what number or percent of cases fall above or below a given score or between two given scores

c. Given the general problem with $\underline{M}=\underline{X}$, $\sigma=\underline{Y}$, determine what the percentile rank of a given score is

d. Given the general problem with $\underline{M}=\underline{X}$, $\sigma=\underline{Y}$, determine what Px is

e. Find the distance in σ units any score is from the mean, with a 95 percent standard of accuracy.

Secondary — Psychology

TBO–27. Learner is to evaluate his own social values in relation to community norms, peer expectations and law so that he can:

    a. List statements of his own social values, how he perceives his peers' values and how he perceives the values of his community

    b. List where his values are in conflict with those of his peers and that of his community as in a (above)

    c. Describe in writing his perception of how his values may or may not lead to conflict with other individuals

    d. Describe in writing his ideas relating to "whether a person should change his values" giving reasons pro or con

    e. List where his values are in conflict with laws.

Secondary — History

TBO–28. Learner is to develop an integrated, self-designed concept of the causes and consequences of war so that he can:

    a. Choose any of six major wars and research them to the degree that he can compile a list of causes and consequences for each based on recorded facts or expert opinion

    b. Summarize his findings and write a conclusion based on the evidence compiled.

Secondary — Political Science

TBO–29. Learner is to understand the concept of "individual rights and freedom" so that he can:

    a. List the constitutional provisions relating to individual rights

    b. Write a paragraph describing the history of and current status of one of these topics

      1) gun possession

      2) wire tapping

      3) use of social security number

      4) bail laws

    c. Research his state laws relative to rights to *due process of law* for juveniles and juvenile-parent relationships

    d. Write a paper explaining his perception of how and why a person must assume individual responsibility along with the enjoyment of individual freedom

    e. Investigate and answer this question: Do we have free public education in the United States?

    f. Devise a list of individual actions or behaviors necessary for the protection of his freedom in a democracy.

Secondary — Economics

TBO–30. Learner is to understand the concept of inflation and possible methods for its control so that he can:

    a. Outline the major provisions of our labor legislation relating to collective bargaining

    b. Write a judgement statement relative to labor's responsibility, if any, in regard to wage demands

    c. Write a judgement statement relative to industry's responsibility, if any, in regard to wage demands

    d. List the available presidential powers that relate to wage and price control

e. Outline the national legislation relative to fiscal controls
    for dealing with inflation
f. Outline the national legislation relative to the operation of
    the stock market
g. Write a short paper explaining how governments (federal,
    state, local) can stimulate or retard inflationary trends
h. Explain (in a paragraph or two) how deficit spending
    is related to inflation
i. Graph the income-expenditure figures for the federal gov-
    ernment for the years 1910-70. How many years showed
    a balanced budget?—a surplus?—a debt? Write a short
    explanation of your position, and the reasons for it, rela-
    tive to a balanced budget
j. Make a list of the total effects of inflation on our country.

Appendix A

Answers to Criterion Test — Sections 2 and 3, page 8

1.	G		8.	I
2.	I		9.	G
3.	G		10.	T
4.	I		11.	G
5.	G		12.	I
6.	T		13.	T
7.	I		14.	I

A-2

Key to Self Check Test — Section 4, pages 19-20.

1.	Yes	(No)	1	(2)	3
2.	Yes	(No)	1	(2)	(3)
3.	Yes	(No)	1	2	(3)
4.	(Yes)	No	1	2	3
5.	Yes	(No)	(1)	2	3
6.	(Yes)	No	1	2	3
7.	Yes	(No)	(1)	(2)	(3)
8.	(Yes)	No	1	2	3
9.	Yes	(No)	(1)	(2)	3
10.	(Yes)	No	1	2	3

A-3

Answers to Self Check Test — pages 28-29.

Your answer, by way of describing each of the four classes in the COGNITIVE DOMAIN, should differ from the wording below, but the general ideas expressed should be the same.

Class 1. **Knowledges.** K's are low level information or facts such as names, dates, etc., and probably the least important class of objectives.

Class 2. **Understandings.** U's are more important than K's as they deal with generalizations, concepts, principles and applications.

Class 3. **Processes.** P's are specific mental skills as classifying, abstracting, associating, measuring, generalizing and evaluating; generally used in problem solving.

Class 4. **Strategies.** S's are two or more processes put together as a plan or a method as used in problem solving.

A-4

Answers to Self Check Test — pages 32-33.

Part I. Your answers may not be just like those provided here but should be close, similar or mean the same thing.

1. **Attitude**—an attitude is a mood, a conviction, a belief or a persistent disposition to act in a definable way toward a person, thing or event.

2. **Appreciation**—an appreciation is the perceiving of the worth of an object or event or recognition of the aesthetic value of an object or event.

3. **Interest**—interests are expressed desires to do or act, the readiness to do or act or the feelings which accompany actions or events.

Part II. Name of the four classes of objectives in the COGNITIVE DOMAIN.

1. **Knowledges** or **K's.**
2. **Understandings** or **U's.**
3. **Processes** or **P's.**
4. **Strategies** or **S's.**

A-5

Answers to Criterion Test — Section 5, pages 35-36.

Part I.

    A. COGNITIVE DOMAIN

        Type I—Content Area

           Class 1. **K's—Knowledges**

           Class 2. **U's—Understandings**

        Type II—Process Area

           Class 3. **P's—Processes**

        Type III—Problem Solving Area

           Class 4. **S's—Strategies**

    B. AFFECTIVE DOMAIN
        Type IV—Emotional Area
            Class 5. **At's—Attitudes**
            Class 6. **Ap's—Appreciations**
            Class 7. **In's—Interests**
    C. PSYCHOMOTOR DOMAIN
        Type V—Motor Area
            Class 8. **M's—Movements**
            Class 9. **MO's—Movements with objects or tools**
Note: If you just listed the 9 classes, your answer was satisfactory.

Part II.
    1. run 100 yards—**M—movement**
    2. type a letter—**MO—movement with tool**
    3. list the cranial nerves—**K—knowledge**
    4. read and critically analyze—**P—process (analyze)**
    5. express in writing how he believes—**At—attitudes**
    6. name the parts of the camera—**K—knowledge**
    7. compare verbally the philosophy of X with that of Y—**U—understanding**
    8. classify any of laboratory collection of mosquitos—**P—process (classify)**
    9. formulate a hypothesis—**P—process (hypothesize)**
    10. plays golf twice a week—**MO—movement with tools** or an **In—interest**
    11. develop in writing a plan for—**S—strategy**
    12. list the steps for the solution of the problem—**S—strategy**
    13. edit the rough manuscript—**U—understanding**
    14. prove that X equals Y—**U—understanding**
    15. high jump 48″—**M—movement**
    16. judge a dog show—**U—understand** or possibly **Ap—appreciation**
    17. watches TV football each Saturday—**In—interest**
    18. spell the five words—**K—knowledge**
    19. verify using the criteria devised—**S—strategy** or **P—process (evaluate)**
    20. voluntarily purchased art objects—**Ap—appreciation** or **In—interest**

                              A-6
Answers to Criterion Test — Section 7, pages 54-56.

Part I.
    1a. **identify**
    1b. **sort**

    2a. **contrast**
    2b. (none)

    3a. **plot**
    3b. (none)

4a. interpret
4b. verbally explain and verbally summarize
5a. determine
5b. plot

Part II.

| 1a. | C | 2a. | C | 3a. | O | 4a. | C | 5a. | C |
| 1b. | O | 2b. | none | 3b. | none | 4b. | O | 5b. | O |

Part III.
No standard answer possible as you constructed your own.

A-7

Answers to Criterion Test — Section 8, page 64.

1. a. C
    b. O

2. a. C
    b. C
    c. C

3. a. C
    b. C
    c. C
    d. C
    e. C
    f. C
    g. C
    h. O

A-8

Answers to Criterion Test — Section 10, pages 81-82.

(Your answers should reflect ideas similar to those below.)

Five Functions or Purposes of an Objective:
1. **Communicate with learners.** Learners should be aware of the terminal behaviors they are expected to possess. This can be done by giving them a list of the things they are to be able to do at the end of instruction. Learners can't achieve if they don't know what it is they are expected to achieve.

2. **Communicate with other professional people.** Objectives express exactly what is expected of learners and can be used professionally to delineate areas in courses of study, prevent overlap between courses, inform substitute teachers as to the end products of instruction while they are teaching, etc.

3. **Objectives serve as a base for selecting instructional activities.** When the end products of instruction (terminal behavioral objectives) and the instructional strategy (instructional objectives) are specified, the curriculum constructor or teacher can select those activities that are most directly related to the student's achievement. Time consuming nonappropriate busywork is eliminated.

4. **Objectives serve as a base for selecting appropriate evaluation activities.** Implied in specific objectives are the ways in which the behavior is to be measured. Either the primary overt or the secondary overt behavior is to be measured. Covert behaviors cannot be measured directly.

5. **Objectives serve as written expressions of end products** and therefore are public records of what is being taught (learned). Objectives should be worthy of attainment (useful) from either a technological or a philosophical point-of-view.

May all of your objectives be good ones.

A-9

Answers to Criterion Test — Section 11, pages 85-86.

1. Define or tell in your own words what an experience objective is.

   Your answer should be similar to or express the same idea as this:

   An experience objective is a required, structured or non-structured situation participated in by a learner, the learning outcomes of which are unique to the learner; in other words, no specific terminal behaviors have been specified.

2. Briefly describe an experience objective and tell its purpose.

   An experience objective is merely an experience the learner is to participate in, and he gets out of the experience whatever he can—the outcomes are unique to the learner. Instructors require the experience because it is felt (estimated or concluded) to be a valuable activity. However, if specific behaviors were to be specified it might prevent some learners acquiring some behaviors or the range of possible outcomes is so great and varied that it would be impractical to list them.

Appendix B

The Nine Classes of Behaviors with Synoptic, Related
or Subcategory Terms and Associated Behaviors (Actions)

Class 1. Knowledges (K's):

a. facts	c. dates	e. parts
b. names	d. events	h. information
f. low order concepts	g. low order associations	

1. abbreviates	22. gets	43. names	64. says
2. alphabetizes	23. gives	44. notes	65. selects
3. arranges	24. groups	45. offers	66. separates
4. bisects	25. guides	46. omits	67. shortens
5. cancels	26. holds	47. picks	68. shows
6. checks	27. hunts	48. places	69. sketches
7. chooses	28. identifies	49. points to	70. sorts
8. circles	29. includes	50. positions	71. spells
9. cites	30. increases	51. prints	72. starts
10. copies	31. indicates	52. pronounces	73. states
11. counts	32. informs	53. provides	74. stops
12. crosses out	33. inserts	54. puts	75. takes
13. decreases	34. joins	55. quotes	76. tallies
14. defines	35. labels	56. recites	77. tells
15. describes	36. leaves out	57. records	78. touches
16. deletes	37. lengthens	58. relates	79. transfers
17. designates	38. lets	59. removes	80. underlines
18. divides	39. lists	60. repeats	81. writes
19. encircles	40. locates	61. replaces	
20. finds	41. marks	62. resets	
21. fits	42. matches	63. returns	

Class 2. Understandings (U's):

a. high order concepts
b. comprehension
c. complex relationships

1. applies	7. defines	13. edits	19. integrates
2. appraises	8. demonstrates	14. editorializes	20. interprets
3. computes	9. designs	15. evaluates	21. plans
4. constructs	10. differentiates	16. explains	22. proves
5. contrasts	11. discriminates	17. formulates	23. solves
6. criticizes	12. distinguishes	18. generates	24. uses

Class 3. Processes (P's):

a. analysis

1. breaks down	5. examines	9. simplifies
2. disassembles	6. extracts	10. takes part
3. dissects	7. investigates	
4. divides	8. separates	

b. synthesis (more powerful than term associate)

1. assembles	9. creates	16. puts together
2. blends	10. develops	17. recombines
3. builds	11. fashions	18. reconstructs
4. combines	12. integrates	19. reorders
5. compiles	13. makes	20. reorganizes
6. completes	14. organizes into whole	21. restructures
7. composes		22. structures
8. constructs	15. produces	23. systematizes

c. classify (more powerful than just to know)

1. arranges	8. identifies	16. regroups
2. catalogues	9. indexes	17. renames
3. categorizes	10. isolates	18. reorders
4. chooses	11. orders	19. selects
5. gathers together	12. organizes	20. sequences
	13. patterns	21. sorts
6. grades	14. places	22. tallies
7. groups	15. rearranges	

d. perceive

1. becomes aware of	6. pictures meaning of	9. writes explanation of
2. comprehends	7. gives meaning to	10. orally explains
3. grasps meaning of	8. understands purpose	11. gives significance to
4. sees, mentally		
5. observes		

e. remember

1. defines	9. pictures	17. restates
2. describes	10. portrays	18. retells
3. displays	11. recalls	19. rewrites
4. draws	12. recapitulates	20. shows
5. explains	13. reconstructs	21. summarizes
6. expresses	14. reports	22. tells
7. illustrates	15. rephrases	23. verbalizes
8. lists	16. reproduces	24. writes

f. abstract

1. pictures, mentally
2. represents, apart from
3. thinks, apart from

g. discriminate

1. compares
2. contrasts
3. detects
4. distinguishes
5. recognizes, differences
6. recognizes, likenesses

h. conceptualize (less powerful than create)

1. conceives
2. concludes
3. concocts
4. designs mentally
5. dreams up
6. envisages
7. evolves
8. fabricates mentally
9. forms an idea
10. forms in mind
11. formulates
12. generalizes
13. infers

i. evaluate

1. appraises
2. assays
3. assesses
4. calculates value of
5. decides
6. determines value of
7. determines worth of
8. grades
10. rejects
11. ranks
12. rates
13. weighs

j. translate

1. alters
2. briefs
3. changes
4. condenses
5. converts
6. decodes
7. depicts
8. describes
9. diagrams
10. digests
11. distills
12. encodes
13. epitomizes
14. expands
15. extracts
16. interprets
17. modifies
18. pantomimes
19. paraphrases
20. pictures
21. renders
22. rephrases
23. represents
24. restates
25. retells
26. revises
27. rewords
28. rewrites
29. simplifies
30. simulates
31. sketches
32. substitutes
33. transfers
34. transforms
35. transposes

k. create (more powerful than conceptualize)

1. composes
2. develops
3. discovers
4. fabricates
5. invents
6. writes
7. originates
8. pieces together

l. estimate

1. approximates
2. infers

m. predict

1. anticipates
2. deduces
3. extrapolates
4. forecasts
5. projects

n. associate

1. combines
2. groups
3. joins
4. links
5. matches
6. pairs
7. places together
8. relates
9. unites

o. measure

1. calculates
2. delimits
3. determines
4. limits
5. quantifies
6. weighs

p. theorize

1. hypothesizes
2. postulates

Class 4.   Strategies (S's):

a. plans
b. models
c. schemes
d. systems
e. series
f. strategies
g. problem solving

1. checks, by plan or criteria
2. conducts, as an experiment
3. devises, according to plan
4. invents
5. produces, step by step
6. proves, step by step
7. tests
8. verifies, by plan or criteria
9. investigates
10. discovers, following logical plan

Class 5.   Attitudes (At's):

a. attitudes
b. beliefs
c. convictions
d. likings
e. purposes
f. values

1. accepts
2. accumulates (information)
3. adopts
4. advocates
5. argues
6. asks
7. assumes
8. attempts
9. attends
10. berates
11. bothers
12. challenges
13. checks
14. chooses
15. completes
16. consoles
17. consults
18. criticizes
19. defends
20. disproves
21. disputes
22. enjoys
23. evaluates
24. gathers (data)
25. hates
26. holds (opinions)
27. initiates
28. inveigles
29. investigates
30. involves (himself)
31. joins
32. judges
33. likes
34. loves
35. obeys
36. objects (verbal)
37. offers
38. organizes
39. participates
40. permits
41. perseveres
42. persists
43. promotes
44. proposes
45. praises
46. qualifies (point-of-view)
47. queries
48. questions
49. recommends
50. rectifies
51. rejects
52. repeats (actions)
53. seeks
54. sees (worth or value)
55. shares
56. specifies
57. submits
58. suggests
59. supports
60. sustains
61. tests
62. tolerates
63. views
64. volunteers
65. watches

Class 6.   Appreciations (Ap's):

a. values
b. esteems
c. sympathizes

(Many of the behaviors listed under **Attitudes** will serve here.)

Class 7.   Interests (In's):

a. motives
b. desires
c. incentives
d. impulses

(Many of the behaviors listed under **Attitudes** will serve here.)

Class 8.   Movements (without objects or tools) (M's):

a. movements
b. motions
c. skills
d. acts
e. actions

1. arches
2. bends
3. chases
4. climbs
5. clutches
6. crawls
7. follows
8. grabs
9. grasps
10. grips
11. hits
12. hops
13. jumps
14. kicks
15. knocks
16. leans

17. leaps
18. lifts
19. marches
20. nods
21. pitches
22. plucks
23. presses
24. pulls
25. pushes
26. reaches
27. rolls
28. runs
29. shakes
30. sits
31. skips
32. slides

33. somersaults
34. squeezes
35. stands
36. steps
37. stretches
38. swats
39. swims
40. swings
41. taps
42. tosses
43. twists
44. walks
45. waves
46. wiggles

Class 9.   Movements (with objects or tools) (MO's):

a. movements
b. skills
c. arts
d. crafts
e. acts
f. actions

1. bats
2. brushes
3. builds
4. carves
5. catches
6. chisels
7. colors
8. constructs
9. copies
10. covers
11. cuts
12. dabs
13. dots
14. draws
15. drills
16. folds
17. hammers
18. heats
19. holds

20. kicks
21. letters
22. melts
23. mixes
24. molds
25. nails
26. numbers
27. paints
28. pastes
29. pins
30. planes
31. polishes
32. pours
33. punches
34. reams
35. rides
36. rolls
37. rules
38. sands

39. saws
40. scrapes
41. sculpts
42. shakes
43. skates
44. sketches
45. skis
46. smoothes
47. stamps
48. sticks
49. stirs
50. tosses
51. traces
52. trims
53. types
54. uncovers
55. wipes
56. wraps
57. writes

Appendix C

A. COGNITIVE DOMAIN (Content and Processes of that which can be perceived)

   Type I.   Classes of Behavioral Products (Content Area)

            Class 1. Factual knowledge (K's) (low order entities as facts and information)

            Class 2. Understandings (U's) (high order entities as concepts, laws, principles, generalizations)

   Type II.   Class of Behavioral Products (Process Area)

            Class 3. Processes (P's) (transformational entities used in learning and communication)

                   a. Analyzing
                   b. Synthesizing-Integrating
                   c. Classifying-Ordering
                   d. Perceiving-Sensing
                   e. Remembering-Recalling
                   f. Abstracting-Imagining
                   g. Discriminating-Comparing-Distinguishing
                   h. Conceptualizing-Hypothesizing-Theorizing
                   i. Evaluating-Judging-Appraising
                   k. Creating-Inventing
                   l. Estimating-Approximating
                   m. Predicting-Forecasting-Inferring
                   n. Associating-Relating
                   o. Measuring-Quantifying

        p. Generalizing
        q. Translating

Type III.   Class of Behavioral Products (Problem Solving Area)
        Class 4. Strategies (S's) (Plans and skills as entities used in problem solving)
            a. Formal
            b. Informal

B. AFFECTIVE DOMAIN (Emotional and Feeling)

Type IV.   Classes of Behavioral Products (Emotional Area)
        Class 5. Attitudes (At's) (Moods, convictions or persistent dispositions to act entities)
        Class 6. Appreciations (Ap's) (A sensitive awareness or perception of worth entities)
        Class 7. Interests (In's) (Expressed desire to attend to or readiness to attend to entities)

*C. PSYCHOMOTOR DOMAIN (Motor sets and skills)

Type V.   Classes of Behavioral Products (Motor Area)
        Class 8. Movements (M's) (Movements of body or physical actions without involvement of outside objects or tools)
            a. Strength
            b. Speed
            c. Impulsion
            d. Precision
            e. Coordination
            f. Flexibility
        Class 9. Movements with Objects (MO's) (Movements, actions or skills involving objects or tools)

Summary of Five Types and Nine Classes of Objectives

A. COGNITIVE DOMAIN

Type I.
        Class 1. K's — Knowledges
        Class 2. U's — Understandings

*Guilford, J. P., "A System of Psychomotor Abilities." *American Journal Psychology,* 1958, Vol. 71, pp. 164-174.

Type II.
>Class 3. P's — Processes

Type III.
>Class 4. S's — Strategies

B. AFFECTIVE DOMAIN

Type IV.
>Class 5. At's — Attitudes
>Class 6. Ap's — Appreciations
>Class 7. In's — Interests

C. PSYCHOMOTOR DOMAIN

Type V.
>Class 8. M's — Movements without objects or tools
>Class 9. MO's — Movements involving objects or tools

Class 1. Knowledges (K's)
> A. Knowledge is the ability to recall specifics, as facts; lower order principles or concepts; and simple organized sets, as patterns, forms and structures.
> B. Knowing is measured by simple recall types of behavioral situations such as:
>> 1. Listing
>> 2. Reciting
>> 3. Furnishing an example
>> 4. Simple associating as in matching x with y
>> 5. Identifying as by name, place, or pointing to, underlining, encircling, etc.
>> 6. Reproducing symbols
>> 7. Naming or listing a simple sequence of events
>> 8. Labeling the parts of, as from a map or diagram.
> C. Examples of knowledge objectives:
>> 1. The learner is to know how to spell twenty technical terms in chemistry (see list) so that he can spell eighteen out of the twenty correctly from oral dictation.
>> 2. The learner is to know the ten principal river systems of North America and be able to locate them on a map so that when given a blank diagrammatic map of the North American continent he can sketch eight of the ten major rivers in their approximate locations and label them correctly.

Class 2. Understandings (U's)
> A. Understanding is the comprehension or apprehension of general relations to particulars in high order events; of making experience intelligible by bringing perceived particulars under appropriate higher order concepts; or the ability to use ideas in functional settings.
> B. Understanding is measured by behaviors requiring actions over and above mere recall such as:

1. Assemblying, as the sequence of complex events detailing the directions for repairing an automobile motor
2. Taking apart, as describing the exact nature of the particles composing a particular atom
3. Applying the principles of hydraulics to the design of a flood control dam
4. Judging the worth (acceptance or rejection) of a machine involving the testing of the machine and comparing performance to a set of standards
5. Relating rules to observed actions, as in refereeing a basketball game
6. Interpreting observed phenomena and generalizing it into a theory, principle, law or concept
7. Designing a new or useful form pattern or object to achieve a desired purpose, to conform to a set of specifications or to incorporate appropriate elements
8. Comparing ideas, objects or events in comprehensive fashion to achieve a desired goal—as to clarify or confirm
9. Classifying an object or event by means of a system, or a set of objects or events using a set of criteria
10. Translate from one form to another as from language to language or ideas to actions.

C. Examples of understanding objectives:
1. The learner is to develop an understanding of 35-mm color slide photograph so that when given X equipment or items he can expose a roll of Y film, develop it, mount the slides and project them for viewing (all actions and/or products conforming to Z specifications).
2. The learner is to develop an understanding of the role Micronesia plays in current world affairs so that he can:
   a. Trace the economic development of the island group since the end of WWII and predict its status in 1975 and in 1980.
   b. Relate Micronesia's present state of sovereignty to hypothetical proposals for colonial, commonwealth and trustee status through descriptive statements of pros and cons as probably perceived by the indigenous population.
   c. Describe Micronesia's ability to protect its political and sovereign states assuming X (a set of conditions).
   d. Devise an outline plan, using concrete examples, for its potential economic development during the five-year period, 1970-75.

Class 3. Processes (P's)

A. Processes are specific mental skills which are any of a set of actions, changes, treatments or transformations of Classes 1, 2, 5, 6 or 7, entities generally used in a strategy following a special sequence to achieve the solution of a problem associated with the learning act, the use of learning products or the communication of things learned.

B. Processes are measured by placing the learner in a unique problem situation which requires him to demonstrate a defined behavior describing a given process such as:
  1. Analyzing—given a known or unknown object or event, the object or event is broken down into its component parts to a specific degree.
  2. Synthesizing—given a known or unknown set of subparts, a unit is composed having a known or new form, pattern or function not previously present.
  3. Classifying—categorizing, on some given basis or using a given set of criteria, of one or more objects or events using some feature or features of the object or event in the process, or the creation of a set of criteria for categorizing two or more objects or events.
C. Examples of process objectives:
  1. The learner is to develop skill in translating German into English so that he can write in English a reasonable and clear equivalent form of a German short story of not less than 500 nor more than 750 words within 30 minutes using a German-English dictionary as needed.
  2. The learner is to develop skill in conceiving the correct three-dimensional forms of objects depicted as two-dimensional schema (unfolded solids) so that when presented with ten sketches he can either draw or describe the correct three-dimensional object represented.

Class 4. Strategies (S's)
A. Strategies are heuristic entities or methods which result from either the art or skill utilized in devising or employing specific processes as a plan in a special order to achieve a definable goal, usually the solution to a problem associated with the learning act, using learning products or communicating about things learned.
B. Strategies, or rather the ability to devise and/or use them, are measured in problem-solving situations requiring the application of two or more processes and an acceptable problem solution. Behaviors requiring proofs or the ability to describe a method to accomplish a goal may indicate the ability to devise and/or use a strategy.
C. Examples of strategy learning objectives:
  1. The learner is to plan and build a twelve foot rowboat which will transport five individuals or a load of 1,000 pounds, leaving a five-inch draft from boat to waterline, and in the execution of the project furnish in order:
    a. a set of working drawings
    b. a list of materials
    c. an item-cost projection
    d. a construction time projection
    e. the finished product.
  2. The learner is to devise a method for and report on the comparative effectiveness of achievement of two groups of

learners (N 20) each group learning to spell by a different method of instruction.

3. The learner is to hypothesize a strategy for devising a valid instructional system suited to training retail food store cashier-checkers. The strategy is to be presented as a written report complete with appropriate charts and diagrams.

4. The learner is to prove the congruence of any three triangles by detailed logical analysis so that when given a set of three triangles, he can describe in writing a complete, correct proof within five minutes.

Class 5. Attitudes

A. An attitude is a feeling, mood, value or conviction; or a persistent disposition to act in a definable way toward a person, thing or event.

B. Attitudes are at best rarely measured validly or reliably. Some value and attitude scales or devices exist but much more scientific investigation of this field is needed. Attitudes are not divorced from cognitive and phychomotor entities. For example, our perception of another person—our knowledge of his habits, likes, dislikes, physical features, and our understanding of his personality and behavior patterns—often leads to like or dislike; a feeling which may or may not be exhibited overtly. Behaviors clearly and specifically associated with a given attitude remain to be discovered and identified.

C. Examples of attitude objectives. Since attitude behaviors have not been delineated for specific attitudes it is difficult, if not impossible, to define behavioral objectives. For example, pain, as expressed by facial expression, could be the result of or a response to external trauma, internal physiological malfunction, self-depreciation or dissatisfaction with the observed or described behavior of others. Considering these several possibilities, the behavior—expressing pain—could hardly be listed as a behavior indicating acceptance or rejection of another person; yet, it might be. In other words, what is one *doing* when he is *accepting* or *rejecting?* It would be difficult to answer this question in behavioral terms.

The above should not be taken as saying that behaviors cannot be listed, nor should one conclude that the task is impossible. Obviously more research is needed; but, in the meantime, attempts at listing behaviors should be made. Using our illustration of attitude associated with *acceptance* or *rejection* we might suggest behaviors such as:

1. Presence, absence and content of remarks made by a person to others indicating acceptance or rejection
2. The degree to which a person socializes with others
3. Scores obtained through using rating scales
4. Volunteering to do or participate in
5. Successful completion of work or a project done on "one's own"

6. Persistent behavior conforming to a given model

7. Willingness to "stand up" for a view or course of action.

These behaviors may in some way be related to acceptance or rejection, yet they would all be open to question and in total may not be considered as adequately descriptive of the attitude in question. They might, at best, constitute a beginning, perhaps opening the door to finding other behaviors. In this sense, and to this degree it is helpful to "do the best you can" with attitude behaviors even if what you do is far from perfect.

Class 6. Appreciations

A. An appreciation is the sensitive awareness or perception of the worth of an object or event or the recognition of the aesthetic value of an object or event.

B. Appreciations, like attitudes, are at best rarely measured validly or reliably. Some appreciation tests are available, as in Art. However, an examination of these appreciation tests reveal that many of the test items appear to measure *Knowledges* rather than *Appreciations*. The problem again is one of asking the question: What is one *doing* when he is *appreciating?* If one cannot decide exactly what human behaviors are associated specifically with appreciating then it is difficult to claim we are teaching an "appreciation." That is, there is no behavioral proof—no way of measuring the presence or absence of the appreciation. The answer does not rest with *teaching only those entities for which behaviors can be identified.* If this restrictive approach were decided on, then much of what is paramount in and to our culture would be eliminated from education. Attitudes, appreciations and interests are acquired (learned) even if we know little about them. Not only are they learned, but they are important behaviors to acquire.

Again, as with attitudes, the thing to do in listing appreciation behaviors, is to "do the best you can even if it is far from perfect." We have to start somewhere!

C. As with attitudes, appreciation behaviors are difficult if not impossible to define. Consequently you can only do your best in attempting to write objectives. Suggestions of profitable approaches are:

1. Ascertaining if individual is aware of basic elements considered by authorities to be significant in some area of art, music, drama, personal relations, etc.

2. Ascertaining if individual can express his feelings about some area as art, music, personal relations, science, culture, etc.

3. Ascertaining if individual can express his feelings about some given aspect of a broader area as the role of atomic energy in peace and war, the way he views cubism in art, etc.

The problem with listing these behaviors is the fact that we, as educators, can often detect the presence of an appreciation only if we have the person respond in some verbal fashion. We can think of logical, verbal responses which are related to appreciations but other responses are illusive or impractical. Verbal responses, on the other hand, may indicate the presence of behaviors more cognitive than affective in their nature. An example of what is meant can be seen if one attempts to measure an individual's *appreciation of the role of science in daily life.* Asking the learner to list how science is used can result in the learner listing what he has perceived and memorized (remembered) from books, talking to teacher, etc., rather than his true "feelings" about the role of science.

What responses, other than verbal, might be used to measure appreciations? Let's use the field of art as an example and suggest these, although they are open to the question of validity:
1. Number of art books voluntarily purchased
2. Number of art publications voluntarily checked out of library
3. Number of art periodicals subscribed to
4. Frequency of attendance at art lectures, showings, museums, etc.
5. Number and frequency of art purchases for personal possession
6. Frequency of comments about art topics

These behaviors, even if valid, are difficult if not impractical to measure in present-day educational settings. However, they should not be overlooked—they may be potentially significant.

Class 7. Interests

A. Interests are expressed desires or feelings which accompany special attention to objects or events or the readiness to attend to or be moved by objects or events.

B. Interests, like attitudes and appreciations, are difficult to measure validly and reliably; but, there are interest scales available in this area. Most scales force the person to choose (make a verbal commitment) which casts some doubt on the affective nature of the thing being measured—it might have high cognitive overtones, or it could be entirely cognitive. As with other affective behaviors, the handy way to measure interests is to secure verbal responses reflecting the way the individual feels about the area in question. Behaviors other than verbal are frequently elusive, beyond measure or impractical.

C. Examples of interest objectives. Stating objectives of interests is difficult because of our lack of knowledge and understanding of specific one-to-one relationships between observable actions and interests. As with attitudes and appreciations, you can do the best possible for the time being while being alert for new and profitable approaches to the problem.

Behaviors of a verbal or near verbal nature reflecting interests are:

1. Individual selects areas of interest indicated by words or terms as on a rating scale.

2. Individual lists those things he is interested in.
3. Individual chooses between alternatives indicating those of higher comparative interest.
4. Individual responds to structured questions concerning the time he attends to an area, the way he attends to an area, the things he does while attending to some given area or the things he thinks about while attending a given area.

Behaviors of a nonverbal nature which may be associated with interests, although not by themselves proof of interest are:
1. Number of times or the amount of time one attends to or participates in.
2. Length of time attending to correlated with energy expended (working hard for a long time).
3. Degree to which a person goes to attend to (he does it even if it is difficult) or to participate in.
4. Degree to which a person is merely a passive consumer or an active originator. (Watching TV may not indicate any high interest.)

Class 8. Movements (without objects or tools)
A. Movements, body motions or physical skills which are any of a set of motions involving the motor nervous system.
B. Movements are measured directly by performance tests or criteria.
C. Examples of movement (without tools) objectives:
1. The learner is to develop skill in swimming so that he can, using any stroke of his choice, swim fifty meters within two minutes.
2. The learner is to develop coordination and strength so that he can complete forty continuous push ups within sixty-four seconds.

Class 9. Movements (with objects or tools)
A. Movements, body motions or skills which are any of a set of motions involving the motor nervous system and any object, tool or machine.
B. Movements are measured directly by performance tests or criteria.
C. Examples of movement (with tools) objectives:
1. The learner is to develop skill in typing so that, using an IBM Selectric typewriter, he can copy a "rough" manuscript of 287 words, in proper style, within five minutes and with no more than three errors.

Index

Aids, in objectives, 16
Affective behaviors, 37-47, 105
Affective domain, 22-23, 29-32, 108
Affective Domain, defined, 22
Analysis of objective, 50-54
Appreciation behaviors, 31, 105
Appreciations, defined, 30, 113
Appropriateness, of objectives, 150
Attitude behavior, 29-30, 105
Attitudes, defined, 29, 112

Behaviors, in open and closed objectives, 58-59
Behaviors, philosophical usefulness of, 70
Behaviors, technological usefulness of, 70

Closed objectives, 57-63
Closed objectives, examples of, 58
Cognitive domain, 22-28, 107-108
Cognitive domain, defined, 22
Conditions, in objectives, 16
Covert behaviors, 49-50

Domains of behaviors, 22-23, 107-109

Evaluation, in relation to objectives, 68-69, 79-80
Experience objectives, 83-85
Experience objectives, defined, 83
Experience objectives, examples of, 84-85

Goals, 1, 3-4, 10
Goodness, of objectives, 66-74
Goodness, meaning of in objectives, 67-68

Interest, behaviors, 31, 105
Interests, defined, 31, 114
Instructional objectives, 1
Instructional objective, definition of, 6-7

Knowledge behaviors, 23-24, 102
Knowledges, defined, 23, 109

Learning activities, in relation to objective, 67-68, 78-79
Learning, definition of, 14

Middle School objectives, examples of, 89-92
Movement behaviors, 106
Movements, defined, 34, 115
Movements with objects or tools, defined, 34, 115

Objectives, analysis of, 50-54
Objectives, behaviors in, 14-15, 102-106
Objectives, communication function of, 67, 76-78
Objectives, definition of, 4
Objectives, examples of, 87-96
Objectives, open and closed, examples of, 59
Objectives, proper expression of, 11
Objectives, purpose of, 67-70
Objectives, specificity of, 12-13
Open objectives, 57-63
Open objectives, examples of, 58
Overt behaviors, 49-50

Performance goal, 1
Performance objective, 1
Primary behaviors, 49-54

117

Primary school objectives, examples of, 87-89
Processes, defined, 25, 110-111
Processes, list of, 26, 103-104
Process objectives, illustration of, 26, 111
Psychomotor domain, 22-23, 33-34, 108
Psychomotor domain, defined, 23
Psychomotor objectives, illustrations of, 34, 115

Restrictions, in objectives, 16

Secondary behaviors, 49-54
Secondary school objectives, examples of, 92-96
Specific, behavioral objective, 1, 20, 57-58
Specific objective, 1, 20, 57-58

Standards of performance, in objectives, 16
Strategies, defined, 26, 111
Strategy, formal, 27
Strategy, illustration of, 26-27, 111-112

Taxonomy of objectives, 22-35, Appendix C, 107
Terminal behavior, 1
Terminal behavioral objective, 5-6
Time, in objectives, 16

Understanding behaviors, 24, 109-110
Understandings, defined, 23, 109

Validity analysis, of an objective, 70-72
Validity, of objectives, 67